Scott Foresman
SCIENCE

Teacher's Assessment Package
Kindergarten

Scott Foresman

Editorial Offices: Glenview, Illinois • New York, New York
Sales Offices: Reading, Massachusetts • Duluth, Georgia • Glenview, Illinois
Carrollton, Texas • Menlo Park, California

www.sfscience.com

Contributors

Series Authors

Dr. Timothy Cooney
Professor of Earth Science and Science Education
Earth Science Department
University of Northern Iowa
Cedar Falls, Iowa

Michael Anthony Dispezio
Science Education Specialist
Cape Cod Children's Museum
Falmouth, Massachusetts

Barbara K. Foots
Science Education Consultant
Houston, Texas

Dr. Angie L. Matamoros
Science Curriculum Specialist
Broward County Schools
Ft. Lauderdale, Florida

Kate Boehm Nyquist
Science Writer and Curriculum Specialist
Mount Pleasant, South Carolina

Dr. Karen L. Ostlund
Professor
Science Education Center
The University of Texas at Austin
Austin, Texas

Contributing Authors

Dr. Anna Uhl Chamot
Associate Professor and ESL Faculty Advisor
Department of Teacher Preparation and Special Education
Graduate School of Education and Human Development
The George Washington University
Washington, DC

Dr. Jim Cummins
Professor
Modern Language Centre and Curriculum Department
Ontario Institute for Studies in Education
Toronto, Canada

Gale Phillips Kahn
Lecturer, Science and Math Education
Elementary Education Department
California State University, Fullerton
Fullerton, California

Vince Sipkovich
Teacher
Irvine United School District
Irvine, California

Steve Weinberg
Science Consultant
Connecticut State Department of Education
Hartford, Connecticut

ISBN 0-673-59317-7

Copyright © 2000, Addison-Wesley Educational Publishers, Inc.

All rights reserved. The blackline masters in this publication are designed to be used with appropriate equipment to reproduce copies for classroom use only. Scott Foresman grants permission to classroom teachers to reproduce these masters.

Printed in the United States of America

234567890 PO 03 02 01 00 99

Contents

Introduction iv
    Traditional Assessments iv
    Alternative Assessments v
    Performance Tasks v
    Scoring Rubrics v
    Self-Assessment Checklists v

Student Portfolios v
    Introduction v
    Contents of a Portfolio vi
    Selecting Items for the Portfolio vi
    Maintaining the Portfolio vii
    Evaluating the Portfolio vii

Multiple Intelligences viii

	Portfolio Ideas	Wall Charts	Graphic Organizers	Chapter Reviews	Chapter Assessments
Unit A					
Chapter 1	1	2	3	4	5–6
Chapter 2	7	8	9	10	11–12
Chapter 3	13	14	15	16	17–18

	Portfolio Ideas	Wall Charts	Graphic Organizers	Chapter Reviews	Chapter Assessments
Unit B					
Chapter 1	19	20	21	22	23–24
Chapter 2	25	26	27	28	29–30
Chapter 3	31	32	33	34	35–36

	Portfolio Ideas	Wall Charts	Graphic Organizers	Chapter Reviews	Chapter Assessments
Unit C					
Chapter 1	37	38	39	40	41–42
Chapter 2	43	44	45	46	47–48
Chapter 3	49	50	51	52	53–54

	Portfolio Ideas	Wall Charts	Graphic Organizers	Chapter Reviews	Chapter Assessments
Unit D					
Chapter 1	55	56	57	58	59–60
Chapter 2	61	62	63	64	65–66
Chapter 3	67	68	69	70	71–72

Scott Foresman Science Assessment System

National Science Education Assessment Standards
- Assessments must be consistent with the decisions they are designed to inform.
- Achievement and opportunity to learn science must be assessed.
- The technical quality of the data collected is well matched to the decisions and actions taken on the basis of their interpretation.
- Assessment practices must be fair.
- The inferences made from assessments about student achievement and the opportunity to learn must be sound.

Introduction

Every teacher collects information (assesses) while teaching. Teachers listen to children's responses, observe their performance during activities, note cooperation and interaction among children, and identify children who are not involved in the learning process. Teachers are literally "walking, talking assessment machines." Much of this assessment happens informally. This informal assessment data, plus data from more formal assessments, are used to modify instruction and improve learning.

Science teachers are challenged to assess what children know, what children are able to do, and what children value in learning science. Our assessment system provides insights into children's development of conceptual understanding, reinforces productive learning practices, and validates learning activities. Children need frequent, systematic, and consistent feedback to understand their own strengths and capabilities in learning science and to identify areas that need improvement. Our well-designed assessment system helps teachers and children reflect on the learning that has occurred.

The assessment system for *Scott Foresman Science* includes developmentally appropriate tasks that use formats that enable children to demonstrate what they know and what they can do. The assessment system provides teachers with the tools to collect relevant data and information that are consistent, reliable, and valid for all children. The assessments are flexible and adaptable to accommodate a wide variety of learning styles and language proficiencies, empowering children to demonstrate their knowledge and skills in multiple ways.

Traditional Assessments

Written assessments include multiple choice, matching, completion, short answer, and essay. Multiple choice and matching items allow for many children to be assessed in a relatively short time over a wide range of content areas. No materials are needed that require extensive preparation, and the assessments can be scored quickly by hand or machine.

Completion and short-answer items for which children do not choose an option but construct the answer lower the chance of guessing. Children do not react solely to a limited number of options (recognizing one as being a better choice than the others), so misconceptions and partial understanding are more easily identified. Short-answer items are scored by comparing responses to a model response and making decisions about how much credit is to be given.

Essay questions demonstrate children's conceptual understanding and their ability to organize and communicate information.

These questions also reveal children's misconceptions and lower the chance of guessing. In addition, both short-answer and essay items allow for partial credit.

Alternative Assessments

Alternative assessments include any assessment format that is nontraditional, usually requiring child construction, demonstration, or performance. The alternative-assessment formats are child focused, child centered, and authentic. They provide children with opportunities to generate multiple solutions to problems and connect their knowledge to the real world.

In these authentic performance-based assessments, children analyze problems, plan and conduct experiments, gather data, organize their results, and communicate their findings. Children experience and demonstrate the acquisition of inquiry skills through these laboratory investigations. Embedded assessments include extended investigations that take place within a unit or lesson and are linked to specific problems or projects. This assessment format is the most natural and unobtrusive teaching/learning activity. It is the closest to instruction and is realistic, corresponding to how problems are commonly encountered and addressed in the real world.

Alternative assessment strategies used in our elementary science program include story writing, letter writing, advertisements, reflections, game playing, model making, explorations, experiments, investigations, conventions, conferences and debates, applications, and teacher observations. These strategies incorporate reading and language arts skills as well as mathematics skills into the assessment system.

Performance Tasks

Many science inquiry/process skills can only be validly assessed by performance tasks. The *Explore, Investigate, Experiment Activities*, and *Performance-Based Activities* require children to complete an investigation, solve a problem, and conduct an experiment. They are authentic in that they involve children in all phases of research as scientists. This form of assessment task determines if children understand the relevant content and are proficient with inquiry/process skills as well as extending or applying these skills and concepts to new situations.

Scoring Rubrics

Rubrics, which appear in the teacher's Lab Manual in grades 1–6 and in the Teacher's Edition in Kindergarten, are comprehensive evaluations examining children's acquisition of inquiry/process skills and science content as well as communication skills. The rubrics can be presented to the children so they clearly understand what is expected of them. Such detailed, specific feedback on performance is a crucial step toward encouraging children to assess their own performance and achievement.

Self-Assessment Checklists

Checklists reinforce good inquiry/process skill techniques and embed assessment with instruction.

Student Portfolios

Introduction

Developing a good portfolio is more an art than a science. The portfolio assessment includes suggested activities and products for inclusion, an opportunity for indicating why an entry was chosen for inclusion, and guidelines for evaluating the portfolio. The following types of entries are suggested for children's portfolios.

Investigation Entry

The investigation entry requires the child to design, carry out, and report results of an observational and/or experimental process. This is a hands-on investigation or experiment, which focuses on a child-initiated question or problem.

Research Entry
In keeping with the present day emphasis on science for all Americans, the research entry requires children to conduct the kind of research a citizen might do to investigate and solve a problem of personal or societal significance and to make a decision regarding the issue. Such an entry requires identifying legitimate sources of information and accessing, analyzing, synthesizing, and evaluating various pieces of information about a topic. It also encourages the child to identify alternatives and trade-offs and to make a decision based on scientific knowledge and the use of scientific reasoning.

Applications Entry
The applications entry requires the child to use scientific information for a purpose other than research. This entry may be expressive or inventive in nature.

An expressive application allows the child to communicate scientific information in a medium of his or her choice. This may include, but is not limited to, writing a letter to the editor, writing an article for a magazine or newspaper, creating an informative video or pamphlet, or creating a work of art that expresses a scientific concept in a unique manner.

The inventive application allows the child to show how scientific information can be used to solve real-world problems. This may include creating a device that is used to solve a specific problem or constructing a model that demonstrates a scientific principle. The entry must include a written or verbal description of the scientific basis for the entry.

Open Choice Entry
The open choice entry allows the child to submit any piece of classroom work that provides further evidence for any of the four essential parameters. This may include another piece of work that fits into the experimental research, nonexperimental research, or applications of science categories. However, children may submit any piece of work, provided it presents further evidence that is described in the child's reflective summary.

Contents of a Portfolio
There is no prescription for what items should be in a portfolio. Because items selected for a portfolio can take many different forms, many aspects of learning can be documented. Obviously, items should demonstrate growing content knowledge, but equally important items should demonstrate the child's science process skill abilities and even his/her attitudes toward science. Even the child's ability to communicate through writing, drawing, drama, and speaking can be documented. Simply, the portfolio documents content that is learned, skills that are mastered, and attitudes that are displayed.

Scott Foresman Science provides numerous specific suggestions for portfolio items on the Portfolio Ideas page in the Teacher's Assessment Package.

The following is a sample of possible items to consider for inclusion in a portfolio:
- Videotaped presentations
- List of books read
- Audiotaped interviews
- Pictures drawn
- Child testimonials, taped or written
- Data collected
- Test scores and answer sheets
- Graphs
- Photos of experiments or constructions
- Concepts/semantic maps
- Individual or group work
- Copies of awards/prizes
- Performance tasks
- Personal journal excerpts
- Written work in the child's primary language

Selecting Items for the Portfolio
Involving children in the assessment of their achievement and growth is one of the greatest advantages of portfolio assessment. The

selection process is very individual, with each child, under the guidance and recommendation of the teacher, determining what materials to include to tell the "story" of the science they learned and how they learned it. The process encourages children to reflect on their own work, to consider new ideas and their connections to each other and to prior knowledge, and to confront personal feelings and attitudes about the discipline.

Studies by teachers have shown that children need guidance in the selection and reflection process. Strategies such as using class discussions and peer consultation as well as sharing examples of what other children have selected for their portfolio can help children think about their work and its significance.

In addition to children selecting materials, teachers may also choose to place work in the portfolio. This may be particularly important when the teacher wishes to document children's understanding of a particular science concept or their ability to use one or more science process skills. In this way, the portfolio can serve not only as an assessment of individual children, but also as an assessment of the success of the science program, its lessons, and activities.

Maintaining the Portfolio

Because learning is an ongoing process, the items in a portfolio need to be reviewed and updated regularly. Since the portfolio represents the children's science learning, it can be expected that the children assume much of the responsibility for maintaining (selecting and updating) and storing the portfolio just as they are responsible for taking care of textbooks and other school supplies.

While all portfolios will not look alike, teachers need to decide on a container appropriate for the types of items students will be selecting and available classroom storage. Many early childhood teachers (K-2) use large posterboard folders sewn together with yarn, decorated by the children, and stored either flat in a closet or upright in a rack on the counter. Other teachers use letter-sized folders with accordion sides (which can expand from 1 to 3 inches) and store them in crates or special drawers in the classroom file cabinet. Regardless of the container, the contents need to be arranged in a useful manner so both child and teacher can easily review and update the items.

To make the portfolio meaningful for those who read and review it, the teacher can set guidelines for the child, such as:
- include an organized table of contents
- date all work to document growth over time
- provide written descriptions/titles of all drawings, graphs, photos, and so on
- provide a written reflection on the contents of the portfolio

Evaluating the Portfolio

While the individual items within the portfolios can certainly be graded by the teacher, the richness of portfolio assessment lies not on the grade on each item, but instead on the opportunity to display the unique strengths and interest of each child. The focus of portfolio evaluation should be on the broad picture of each child's growth in science content and process over time. This is possible because the portfolio can provide indications of:
- representative work over the evaluation period
- attitudes toward science based on item selection and reflection
- science process skills based on performance samples
- ability to cooperate with others based on group work
- learning styles and preferred learning modalities
- communication skills based on writing samples or tapes

Because the child is involved in selecting items for the portfolio, it is natural for the child to also be involved in presenting the portfolio for review. Teachers are typically planning the portfolio review presentations to correspond with each grading period.

Teacher's Assessment Package

A variety of formats are possible:
- individual conferences with the teacher and/or parent
- sharing with small groups of peers and the teacher
- formal presentations to parents, teachers, and administrators
- formal presentations to small groups of peers and invited community members
- presentations to middle or high school students

In all cases, parents, peers, administrators, older students, or community members evaluate the portfolio and its presentation by providing oral feedback and/or responding to a rating scale typically developed by groups of teachers. The guidelines that the children and teachers used in preparation for their presentations should be shared with the evaluators as they provide a context for assessing the portfolio presentation. Most importantly, feedback, whether oral or on a rating scale, should reflect the broadest desired outcomes of the science program.

Multiple Intelligences/ Learning Styles

In 1983, Howard Gardner of Harvard University directly attacked the idea that intelligence was the same for everyone at all times, arguing instead that "there is persuasive evidence for the existence of several *relatively autonomous* human intellectual competences" (Howard Gardner, *Frames of Mind: The Theory of Multiple Intelligences*, New York: Basic Books, 1993, p 8). As a starting point, Gardner identified seven of these "frames of mind" with the caveat that there may be others. More recently he proposed an eighth intelligence as Naturalist, which has been included here.

Linguistic intelligence involves a sensitivity to the meanings, order, sounds, and rhythms of words. The linguistically intelligent person—like a poet, author, public speaker, or editor—knows how to excite, convince, stimulate, or simply convey information.

Logical-mathematical intelligence stresses logical and abstract thought processes, like those found in good judges, accountants, detectives, and scientists, who can appreciate how things fit together without the need for empirical evidence.

Spatial intelligence is the ability not only to visualize objects and actions but also to change one's perspective of reality while doing so. The architect who can appreciate the appearance of an as yet unconstructed building shows a high degree of spatial intelligence.

Bodily-kinesthetic intelligence involves using the body for functional or expressive purposes. The dancer who can move in the exact same sequence time and time again, and the athlete who knows just how hard or softly to throw a ball are kinesthetically intelligent.

Musical intelligence is a sensitivity to the elements of music—pitch and rhythm—and the ability to appreciate the effects the combinations may induce in someone else. Composers and musicians are musically intelligent.

Interpersonal intelligence is the ability to quickly appreciate the goals, strengths, and weaknesses of others and devise strategies to interact with them in a way pleasing to both. Good teachers, politicians, and friends possess this intelligence.

Intrapersonal intelligence is exhibited by any individual who has an accurate view of him or herself. Those who know exactly what type of job they most like doing are intrapersonally intelligent.

Naturalist intelligence is the capacity to readily recognize flora and fauna, to make other consequential distinctions in the natural world, and to use this ability productively.

Gardner's idea, therefore, prompts us not to ask, "Are our students smart?" but, "How are our students smart?" The more students know that they can be "smart" in these other ways and that they are just as valid as linguistic and logical skills, the greater self-esteem they will carry into their other activities and on into life.

Portfolio Ideas
Unit A Chapter 1

Listed below are items that could be included in students' portfolios for this chapter. The items are categorized by the program component from which they come. Also listed are the main intelligences each item develops. You can use this information to guide students to show their understanding of concepts using their strongest individual problem-solving abilities or intelligences.

These portfolio ideas are only suggestions. You and your students might find other items that demonstrate growing content knowledge, skills development, and attitudes about science.

Component	Item	Intelligence
Teacher's Edition	Pictures from *Topic 1,* pp. A6, A7, A7a, A7b Pictures from *Topic 2,* pp. A9, A9a, A9b Picture from *Chapter Review,* p. A10	Spatial; Naturalist Spatial; Linguistic Spatial; Naturalist
Student Workbook	Living Things I Saw, p. 3 What Living Things Need, p. 4 Nonliving Things in a Home, p. 7 Living or Nonliving?, p. 8	Spatial; Naturalist Spatial; Naturalist Spatial; Naturalist Spatial; Naturalist
Teacher's Assessment Package	Chapter 1 Wall Chart, p. 2 Chapter 1 Graphic Organizer, p. 3 Chapter 1 Review, p. 4 Chapter 1 Assessment, pp. 5–6	Linguistic Linguistic; Spatial Linguistic Linguistic; Logical-Mathematical
Interactive Transparency Package	Interactive Transparency 1	Spatial

Teacher's Assessment Package   Portfolio Ideas **1**

Name _____ Date _____

Wall Chart

Living and Nonliving

K	W	L

2 Chapter 1 Wall Chart   Teacher's Assessment Package

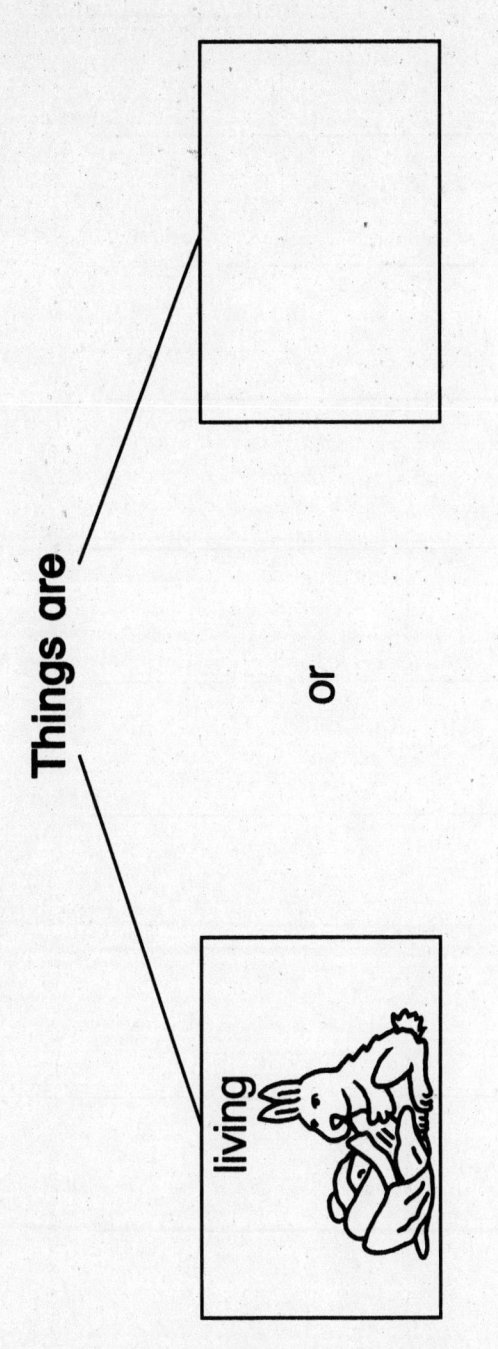

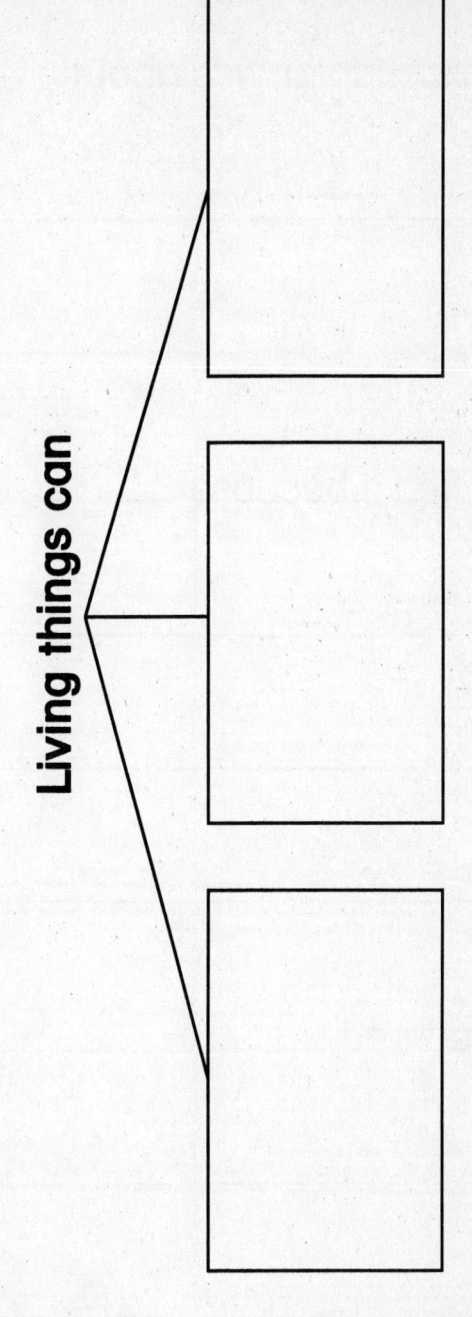

Name _____ Date _____

Graphic Organizer

Things are

or

living

Living things can

nonliving | eat | grow | move

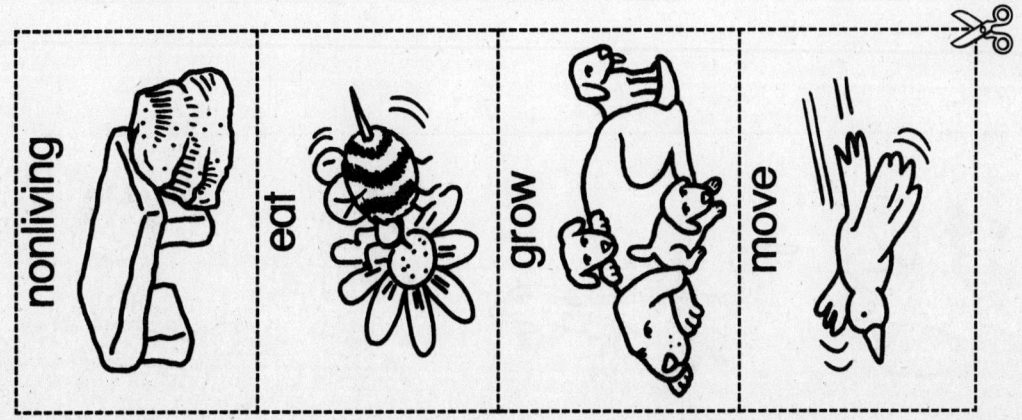

Teacher's Assessment Package

Graphic Organizer **3**

Name _____ Date _____

Chapter 1 Review

This chapter was about _____

_____

_____

I liked it because _____

_____

_____

_____

I learned _____

_____

_____

_____

4 Chapter 1 Review　　　　　　　　　Teacher's Assessment Package

Name _____ Date _____

Chapter 1 Assessment

1. Circle the plant.

2. Circle the animal.

3. Which thing can grow? Color it.

4. Which thing can move on its own? Color it.

5. Which thing can eat? Color it.

Teacher's Assessment Package

Chapter 1 Assessment 5

Name _____   Date _____

6. Circle the living thing.

7. Circle the nonliving thing.

Color the picture that shows what living things need.

8.

9.

10.

6 Chapter 1 Assessment   Teacher's Assessment Package

Portfolio Ideas
Unit A Chapter 2

Listed below are items that could be included in students' portfolios for this chapter. The items are categorized by the program component from which they come. Also listed are the main intelligences each item develops. You can use this information to guide students to show their understanding of concepts using their strongest individual problem-solving abilities or intelligences.

These portfolio ideas are only suggestions. You and your students might find other items that demonstrate growing content knowledge, skills development, and attitudes about science.

Component	Item	Intelligence
Teacher's Edition	Pictures from *Topic 1*, p. A15	Spatial; Linguistic
	Sponge paintings from *Topic 1*, p. A15b	Spatial; Linguistic
	Sentence from *Topic 1*, p. A15b	Linguistic
	Pictures from *Topic 2*, p. A17	Spatial; Linguistic
	Tape recording from *Topic 2*, p. A17a	Linguistic
	Picture from *Topic 2*, p. A17b	Spatial; Linguistic
	Book from *Topic 2*, p. A17b	Logical-Mathematical
	Pictures from *Topic 3*, p. A19	Spatial; Linguistic
	Model from *Topic 3*, p. A19a	Bodily-Kinesthetic; Naturalist
	Picture from *Topic 3*, p. A19b	Spatial
	Counting Book from *Topic 3*, p. A19b	Linguistic; Logical-Mathematical
	Sequence picture from *Topic 3*, p. A19b	Logical-Mathematical
	Pictures from *Chapter Review*, p. A20	Spatial; Naturalist
Student Workbook	How Animals Move, p. 13	Spatial; Linguistic
	Animal Coverings, p. 14	Spatial; Naturalist
	Bird Watch, p. 17	Spatial; Naturalist
	My Pet, p. 18	Spatial; Naturalist
	Animals and Their Babies, p. 21	Spatial; Naturalist
	Caring for Baby Animals, p. 22	Spatial; Linguistic
Teacher's Assessment Package	Chapter 2 Wall Chart, p. 8	Linguistic
	Chapter 2 Graphic Organizer, p. 9	Linguistic; Spatial
	Chapter 2 Review, p. 10	Linguistic
	Chapter 2 Assessment, pp. 11–12	Linguistic; Logical-Mathematical
Interactive Transparency Package	Interactive Transparency 2	Spatial

Name _____ Date _____

Wall Chart

Animals

K	W	L

8 Chapter 2 Wall Chart

Teacher's Assessment Package

Name _____ Date _____

Graphic Organizer

Animals can be covered with
- a shell
- scales

All animals need
- air

feathers | food | fur | water

Teacher's Assessment Package   Chapter 2 Graphic Organizer **9**

Name _____ Date _____

Chapter 2 Review

This chapter was about _____

_____

_____

I liked it because _____

_____

_____

_____

I learned _____

_____

_____

_____

Chapter 2 Review

Teacher's Assessment Package

Name _____ Date _____

Chapter 2 Assessment

1. Circle the animal.

Circle the part that each animal is using to move.

2.

3.

4. Color the animal that is covered by a shell.

5. Color the animal that is covered by fur.

Teacher's Assessment Package   Chapter 2 Assessment   **11**

Name _____ Date _____

6. Circle something that all animals need to live.

7. Color the picture that shows someone giving a pet what it needs to live.

Draw lines to match baby and adult animals.

8.

9.

10. Circle an animal that cares for its babies.

12   Chapter 2 Assessment   Teacher's Assessment Package

Portfolio Ideas
Unit A Chapter 3

Listed below are items that could be included in students' portfolios for this chapter. The items are categorized by the program component from which they come. Also listed are the main intelligences each item develops. You can use this information to guide students to show their understanding of concepts using their strongest individual problem-solving abilities or intelligences.

These portfolio ideas are only suggestions. You and your students might find other items that demonstrate growing content knowledge, skills development, and attitudes about science.

Component	Item	Intelligence
Teacher's Edition	Pictures from *Topic 1*, pp. A25, A25b, A27	Spatial, Logical-Mathematical
	Chart grid from *Topic 1*, p. A25a	Logical-Mathematical
	Seed booklet from *Topic 1*, A25b	Linguistic; Spatial
	Sorting seeds from *Topic 1*, p. A25b	Logical-Mathematical
	Pictures from *Topic 2*, pp. A29, A29b	Spatial; Linguistic
	Pictures from *Topic 3*, pp. A30, A31a, A31b	Spatial; Linguistic
	Leaf rubbing from *Topic 3*, p. A31	Spatial; Kinesthetic
	Picture from *Topic 3*, p. A31a	Logical-Mathematical; Spatial
	See-through book from *Topic 3*, p. A31b	Naturalist; Linguistic
	Trunk rubbing from *Topic 3*, p. A31b	Spatial; Kinesthetic
	Pictures from *Chapter Review*, p. A32	Logical-Mathematical; Linguistic
Student Workbook	A Sunflower Seed Grows, p. 27	Logical-Mathematical
	What Will the Seed Become?, p. 28	Spatial; Naturalist
	What a Plant Needs, p. 33	Spatial; Naturalist
	Helping Plants, p. 34	Spatial; Naturalist
	What Plant Parts Are Missing?, p. 37	Spatial; Naturalist
	Looking at a Leaf, p. 38	Spatial; Kinesthetic
Teacher's Assessment Package	Chapter 3 Wall Chart, p. 14	Linguistic
	Chapter 3 Graphic Organizer, p. 15	Spatial; Linguistic
	Chapter 3 Review, p. 16	Linguistic
	Chapter 3 Assessment, pp. 17–18	Linguistic; Logical-Mathematical
Interactive Transparency Package	Interactive Transparency 3	Spatial

Name _____ Date _____

Wall Chart

Plants

K	W	L

14 Chapter 3 Wall Chart Teacher's Assessment Package

Name _____ Date _____

Graphic Organizer

Plants need
- soil
- air

Plants have
- roots

- water
- stems
- light
- leaves

Teacher's Assessment Package

Chapter 3 Graphic Organizer **15**

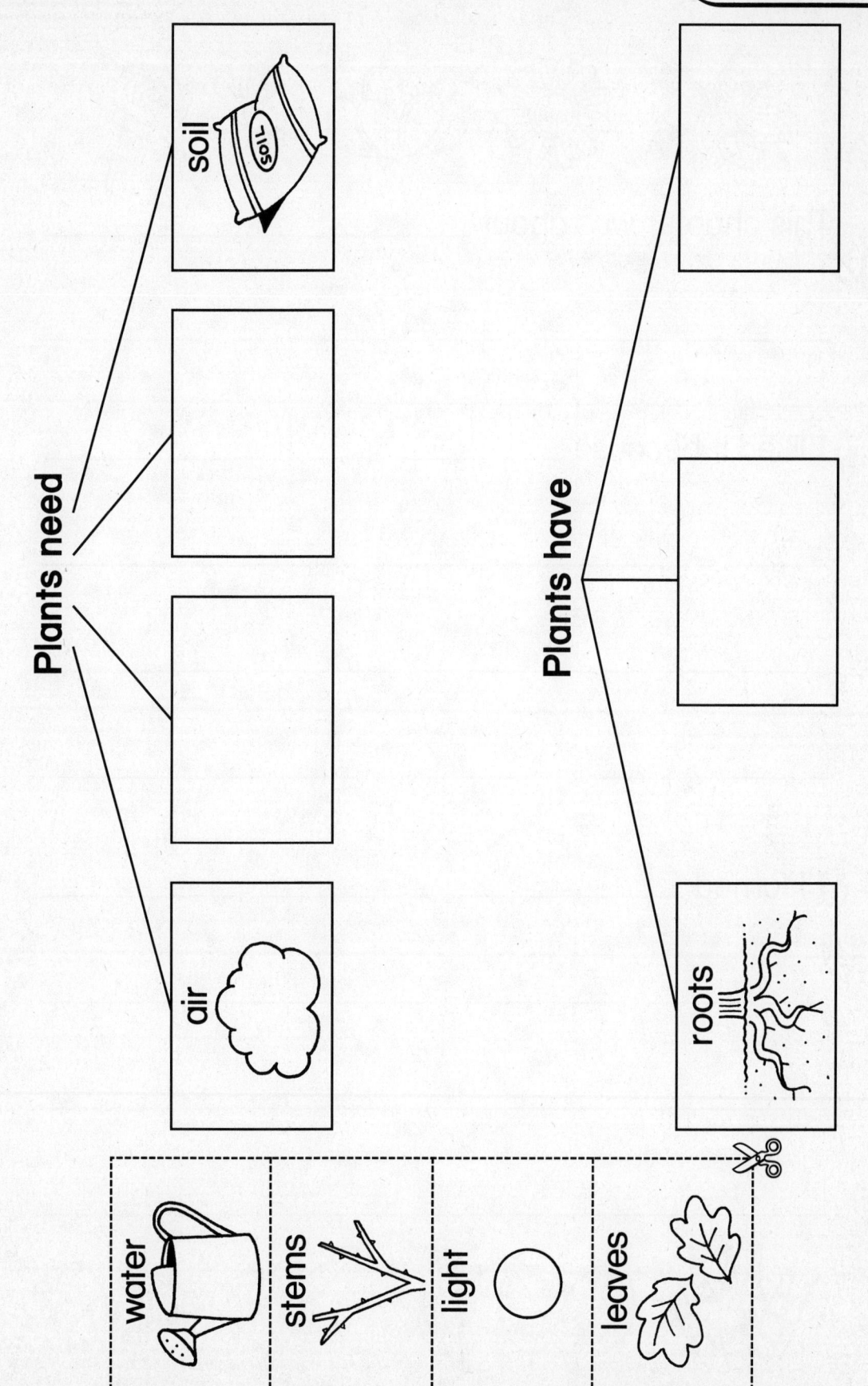

Name _____ Date _____

Chapter 3 Review

This chapter was about _____

_____

I liked it because _____

_____

_____

_____

I learned _____

_____

_____

_____

16 Chapter 3 Review   Teacher's Assessment Package

Name _____ Date _____

Chapter 3 Assessment

1. Color the picture that shows how a bean plant begins.

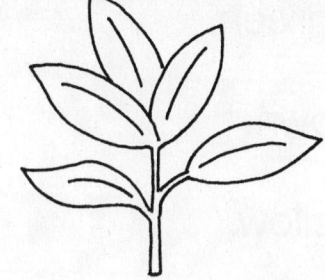

2. Color the picture that shows what these seeds will become.

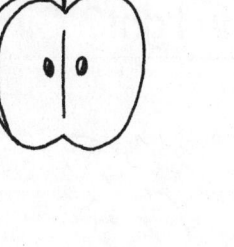

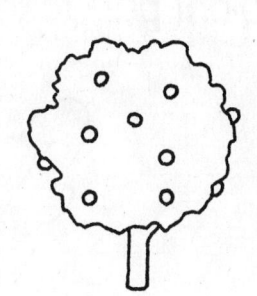

Circle the things that plants need to grow.

3.

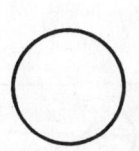

4.

5.

Teacher's Assessment Package   Chapter 3 Assessment **17**

Name _____ Date _____

Look at this plant. Follow the directions.

6. Color the leaves green.

7. Color the root brown.

8. Color the stem yellow.

9. Which plant part takes in light? Circle it.

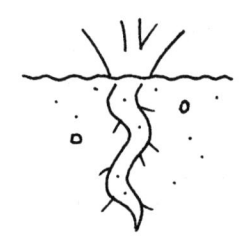

10. Which plant part holds the plant in the soil? Circle it.

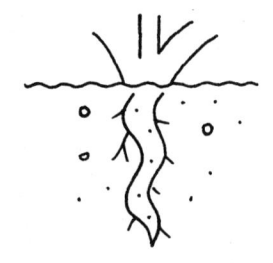

18 Chapter 3 Assessment   Teacher's Assessment Package

Portfolio Ideas
Unit B Chapter 1

Listed below are items that could be included in students' portfolios for this chapter. The items are categorized by the program component from which they come. Also listed are the main intelligences each item develops. You can use this information to guide students to show their understanding of concepts using their strongest individual problem-solving abilities or intelligences.

These portfolio ideas are only suggestions. You and your students might find other items that demonstrate growing content knowledge, skills development, and attitudes about science.

Component	Item	Intelligence
Teacher's Edition	Pictures from *Topic 1*, pp. B7, B7a, B7b	Spatial; Linguistic
	Picture from *Topic 2*, p. B9a	Logical-Mathematical; Spatial
	Picture from *Topic 2*, p. B9a	Spatial; Linguistic
	Booklet from *Topic 2*, p. B9b	Linguistic; Logical-Mathematical
	Paper fold from *Topic 3*, p. B10	Logical-Mathematical; Linguistic
	Puzzle from *Topic 3*, p. B11	Spatial; Logical-Mathematical
	Pictures from *Topic 3*, p. B11, B11a, B11b	Spatial; Logical-Mathematical
	Pictures from *Topic 3*, p. B11b	Spatial; Linguistic
	Collages from *Chapter Review*, p. B12	Logical-Mathematical; Linguistic
	Picture from *Chapter Review*, p. B12	Linguistic; Logical-Mathematical
Student Workbook	All About an Object, p. 43	Spatial; Linguistic
	Sorting It All Out, p. 44	Logical-Mathematical; Spatial
	Light or Heavy?, p. 47	Spatial
	Lighter or Heavier?, p. 48	Spatial; Logical-Mathematical
	What Part Is Missing?, p. 51	Spatial; Logical-Mathematical
	Making a Snack, p. 52	Spatial; Logical-Mathematical
Teacher's Assessment Package	Chapter 1 Wall Chart, p. 20	Linguistic
	Chapter 1 Graphic Organizer, p. 21	Linguistic; Spatial
	Chapter 1 Review, p. 22	Linguistic
	Chapter 1 Assessment, pp. 23–24	Linguistic; Logical-Mathematical
Interactive Transparency Package	Interactive Transparency 4	Spatial

Name _____ Date _____

Wall Chart

Matter

K	W	L

20 Chapter 1 Wall Chart   Teacher's Assessment Package

Name _____ Date _____

Graphic Organizer

Things can be grouped by

- size

Things can be

- heavy

- color
- shape
- light
- hardness

Teacher's Assessment Package

Chapter 1 Graphic Organizer **21**

Name _____ Date _____

Chapter 1 Review

This chapter was about _____

_____

I liked it because _____

_____

_____

_____

I learned _____

_____

_____

_____

Name _____ Date _____

Chapter 1 Assessment

1. Circle the object that is hard.

2. Circle the object that is smooth.

3. Circle the object that is big.

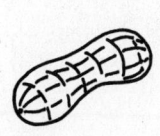

4. Color the group that shows objects with the same shape.

5. Circle the object that belongs in this group.

Teacher's Assessment Package

Name _____ Date _____

6. Color the object that is heavier.

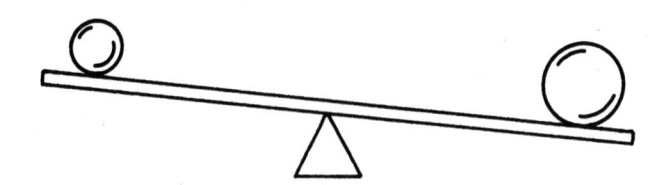

7. Color the object that is lighter.

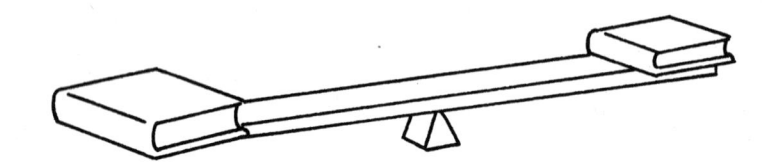

8. Color the object that is heavier than this pen.

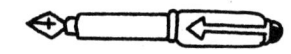

9. Circle the car part that is missing from this car.

10. Circle the part used to steer a bike.

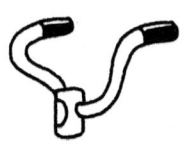

24 Chapter 1 Assessment   Teacher's Assessment Package

Portfolio Ideas
Unit B Chapter 2

Listed below are items that could be included in students' portfolios for this chapter. The items are categorized by the program component from which they come. Also listed are the main intelligences each item develops. You can use this information to guide students to show their understanding of concepts using their strongest individual problem-solving abilities or intelligences.

These portfolio ideas are only suggestions. You and your students might find other items that demonstrate growing content knowledge, skills development, and attitudes about science.

Component	Item	Intelligence
Teacher's Edition	Pictures from *Topic 1*, pp. B17, B17a	Spatial; Logical-Mathematical
	Pictures from *Topic 1*, p. B17b	Linguistic
	Pictures from *Topic 2*, p. B19, B19a	Spatial; Logical-Mathematical
	Group poem from *Topic 2*, p. B19b	Linguistic
	Picture from *Topic 2*, p. B19b	Spatial; Logical-Mathematical
	Picture from *Topic 3*, p. B21	Spatial; Linguistic
	Sunlight on paper from *Topic 3*, p. B21a	Linguistic; Logical-Mathematical
	Paper bag cutouts from *Topic 3*, p. B21b	Spatial; Logical-Mathematical
	Picture from *Topic 3*, p. B23	Spatial; Logical-Mathematical
	Menus from *Chapter Review*, p. B24	Spatial; Logical-Mathematical
	Poster from *Chapter Review*, p. B25	Spatial; Linguistic
Student Workbook	Softer or Louder?, p. 57	Logical-Mathematical
	Canister Shake, p. 58	Logical-Mathematical
	Is It Hot or Cold?, p. 61	Logical-Mathematical
	Changes Caused by Heat and Cold, p. 62	Logical-Mathematical; Spatial
	Inside and Outside Lights, p. 65	Logical-Mathematical; Spatial
	An Important Light, p. 66	Logical-Mathematical; Linguistic
Teacher's Assessment Package	Chapter 2 Wall Chart, p. 26	Linguistic
	Chapter 2 Graphic Organizer, p. 27	Linguistic; Spatial
	Chapter 2 Review, p. 28	Linguistic
	Chapter 2 Assessment, pp. 29–30	Linguistic; Logical-Mathematical
Interactive Transparency Package	Interactive Transparency 5	Spatial

Teacher's Assessment Package

Name _____ Date _____

Wall Chart

Sound, Heat, and Light

K	W	L

Name _____ Date _____

Graphic Organizer

Sounds can be soft or _____

Objects can feel cold or _____

Light can come from fire or _____

✂ hot | sun | loud | lamp

Teacher's Assessment Package

Chapter 2 Graphic Organizer **27**

Name _____ Date _____   Chapter 2 Review

This chapter was about _____

_____

_____

I liked it because _____

_____

_____

_____

I learned _____

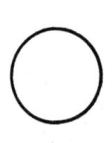

_____

_____

_____

28 Chapter 2 Review   Teacher's Assessment Package

Name _____ Date _____

Chapter 2 Assessment

1. Circle the instrument that makes the louder sound.

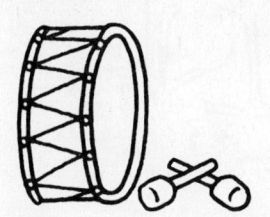

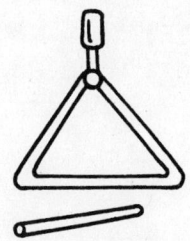

2. Circle the animal that makes the softer sound.

3. Circle the vehicle that makes the loudest sound.

4. Color a food that is hot.

5. Color a food that is cold.

Teacher's Assessment Package

Name _____ Date _____

6. Circle a change caused by heat.

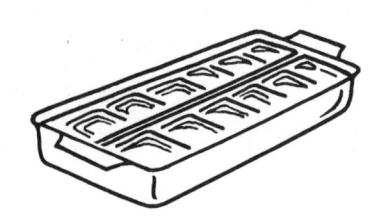

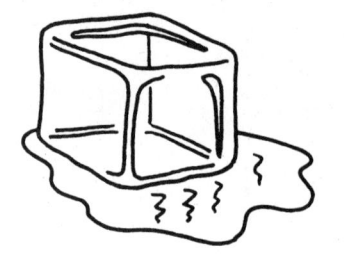

7. Circle a change caused by cold.

8. Color a bright light you could see outdoors.

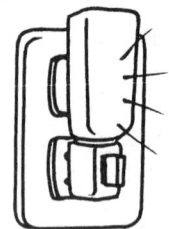

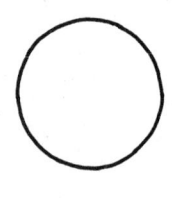

9. Color a light you could use indoors.

10. Color the top light the color that shows you when to stop.

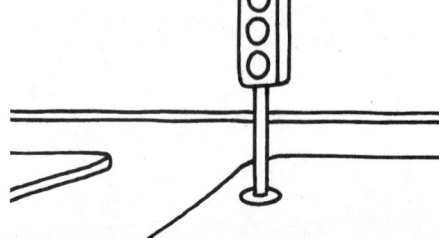

30 Chapter 2 Assessment

Teacher's Assessment Package

Portfolio Ideas
Unit B Chapter 3

Listed below are items that could be included in students' portfolios for this chapter. The items are categorized by the program component from which they come. Also listed are the main intelligences each item develops. You can use this information to guide students to show their understanding of concepts using their strongest individual problem-solving abilities or intelligences.

These portfolio ideas are only suggestions. You and your students might find other items that demonstrate growing content knowledge, skills development, and attitudes about science.

Component	Item	Intelligence
Teacher's Edition	Pictures from *Topic 1*, p. B29	Spatial; Bodily-Kinesthetic
	Pictures from *Topic 1*, p. B29	Spatial; Linguistic
	Recording grid from *Topic 1*, p. B29a	Logical-Mathematical
	Pictures from *Topic 1*, p. B29b	Spatial; Linguistic
	Paper plate turntable from *Topic 1*, p. B29b	Spatial; Kinesthetic
	Pictures from *Topic 2*, p. B31, B31a, B31b	Spatial; Linguistic
	Clay sailboat from *Topic 2*, p. B31b	Spatial
	Pictures from *Topic 3*, p. B33	Spatial
	Pictures from *Topic 3*, p. B33a	Logical-Mathematical
	Magnetic button from *Topic 3*, p. B33b	Spatial; Linguistic
	Magnet fishing pole from *Topic 3*, p. B33b	Logical-Mathematical
	Picture from *Chapter Review*, p. B34	Spatial
Student Workbook	Ways to Move, p. 73	Spatial; Bodily-Kinesthetic
	Ways Toys Move, p. 74	Spatial
	Will It Float or Sink?, p. 77	Spatial; Logical-Mathematical
	Sink the Boat, p. 78	Spatial; Logical-Mathematical
	What Will a Magnet Pull?, p. 81	Spatial; Logical-Mathematical
	What Can a Magnet Pull Through?, p. 82	Spatial; Logical-Mathematical
Teacher's Assessment Package	Chapter 3 Wall Chart, p. 32	Linguistic
	Chapter 3 Graphic Organizer, p. 33	Linguistic; Spatial
	Chapter 3 Review, p. 34	Linguistic
	Chapter 3 Assessment, pp. 35–36	Linguistic; Logical-Mathematical
Interactive Transparency Package	Interactive Transparency 6	Spatial

Teacher's Assessment Package

Name _____ Date _____

Wall Chart

Movement

K	W	L

32 Chapter 3 Wall Chart   Teacher's Assessment Package

Name _____ Date _____

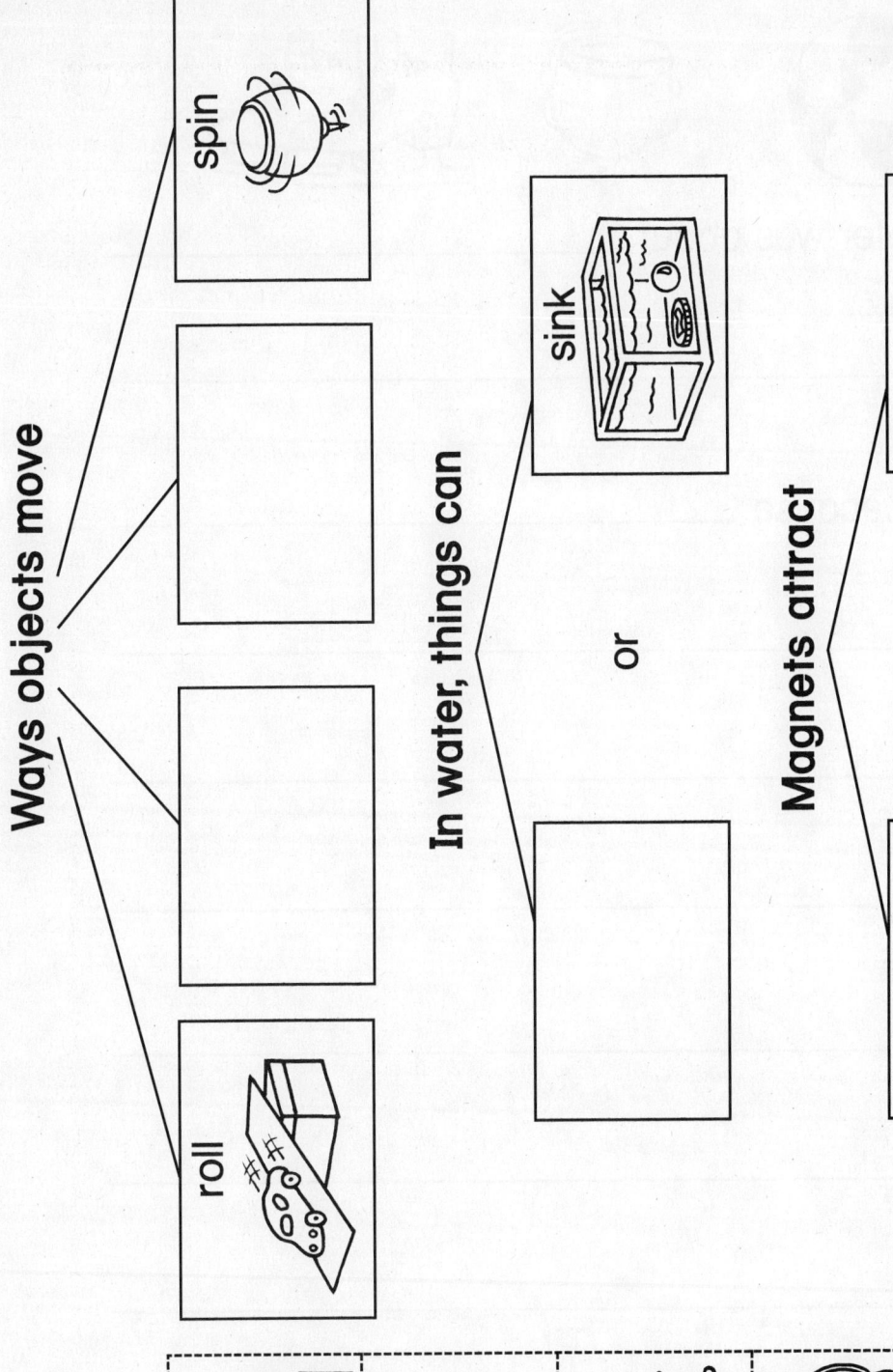

Graphic Organizer

Ways objects move
- spin
- roll

In water, things can
- sink
- or

Magnets attract
- YES
- NO

- float
- bounce
- slide

Teacher's Assessment Package

Chapter 3 Graphic Organizer **33**

Name _____ Date _____

Chapter 3 Review

This chapter was about _____

_____

I liked it because _____

_____

_____

_____

I learned _____

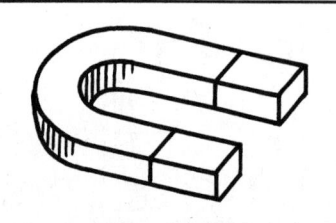

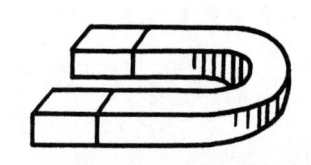

_____

_____

_____

34 Chapter 3 Review

Teacher's Assessment Package

Name _____ Date _____

Chapter 3 Assessment

1. Circle the child who is hopping.

2. Circle the child who is marching.

3. Circle the toy that can roll.

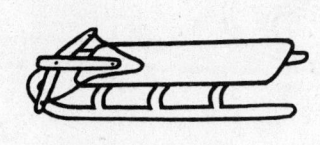

4. Color the toy that can spin.

5. Color the object that will sink.

Teacher's Assessment Package

Chapter 3 Assessment **35**

Name _____ Date _____

6. Color the object that will float.

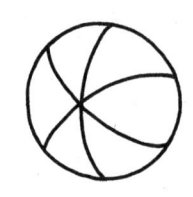

7. Circle the clay shape that will float.

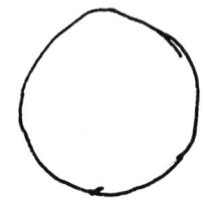

8. Circle the object that a magnet will attract.

9. Circle the object that a magnet will not attract.

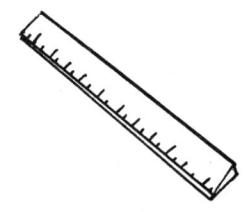

10. Color the picture that shows what happens.

Portfolio Ideas
Unit C Chapter 1

Listed below are items that could be included in students' portfolios for this chapter. The items are categorized by the program component from which they come. Also listed are the main intelligences each item develops. You can use this information to guide students to show their understanding of concepts using their strongest individual problem-solving abilities or intelligences.

These portfolio ideas are only suggestions. You and your students might find other items that demonstrate growing content knowledge, skills development, and attitudes about science.

Component	Item	Intelligence
Teacher's Edition	Pictures from *Topic 1*, p. C7	Spatial; Linguistic
	Clay landform from *Topic 1*, p. C7a	Spatial; Naturalist
	Water flow record from *Topic 1*, p. C7a	Logical-Mathematical
	Picture and sentences from *Topic 1*, p. C7b	Linguistic; Spatial
	Pictures from *Topic 2*, p. C9, C9a	Spatial; Linguistic
	Cloud pictures from *Topic 2*, p. C9b	Spatial; Naturalist
	Pictures from *Topic 3*, p. C11	Spatial; Linguistic
	Flashlight planetarium from *Topic 3*, p. C11	Spatial
	Star pattern model from *Topic 3*, p. C11a	Spatial
	Picture and sentences from *Topic 3*, p. C11b	Linguistic; Spatial
	Picture from *Topic 3*, p. C11b	Spatial; Logical-Mathematical
	Diorama photograph from *Chapter Review*, p. C12	Spatial
	Picture from *Chapter Review*, p. C12	Spatial; Naturalist
	Model from *Chapter Review*, p. C13	Spatial
Student Workbook	Nearby Landforms, p. 87	Spatial; Naturalist
	Visiting a Body of Water, p. 88	Spatial; Naturalist
	Things I Saw in the Daytime Sky, p. 91	Spatial; Naturalist
	My Daytime Activities, p. 92	Spatial
	The Nighttime Sky, p. 95	Spatial; Naturalist
	Daytime and Nighttime, p. 96	Spatial; Naturalist
Teacher's Assessment Package	Chapter 1 Wall Chart, p. 38	Linguistic
	Chapter 1 Graphic Organizer, p. 39	Linguistic; Spatial
	Chapter 1 Review, p. 40	Linguistic
	Chapter 1 Assessment, pp. 41–42	Linguistic; Logical-Mathematical
Interactive Transparency Package	Interactive Transparency 7	Spatial

Teacher's Assessment Package

Earth and Sky

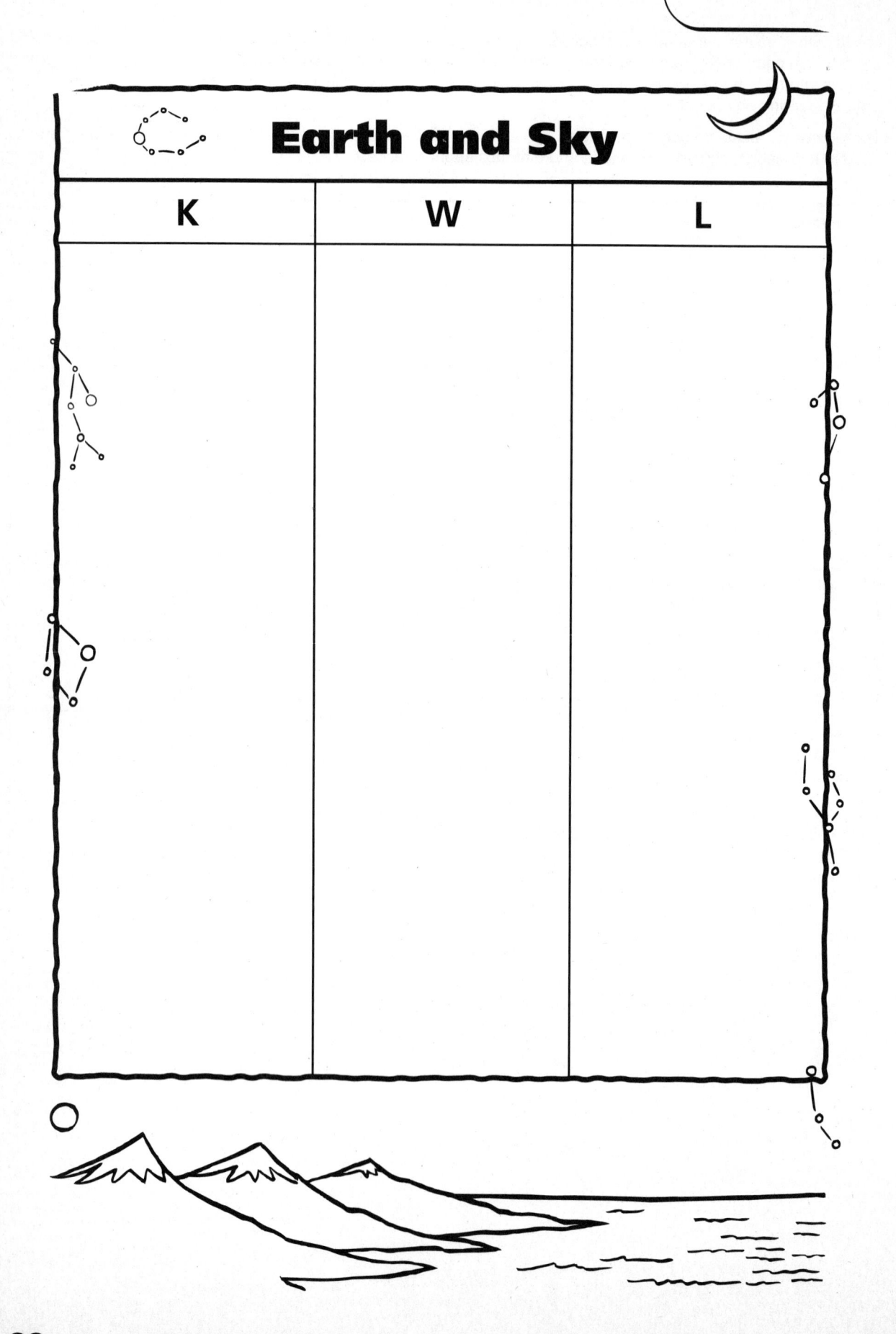

K	W	L

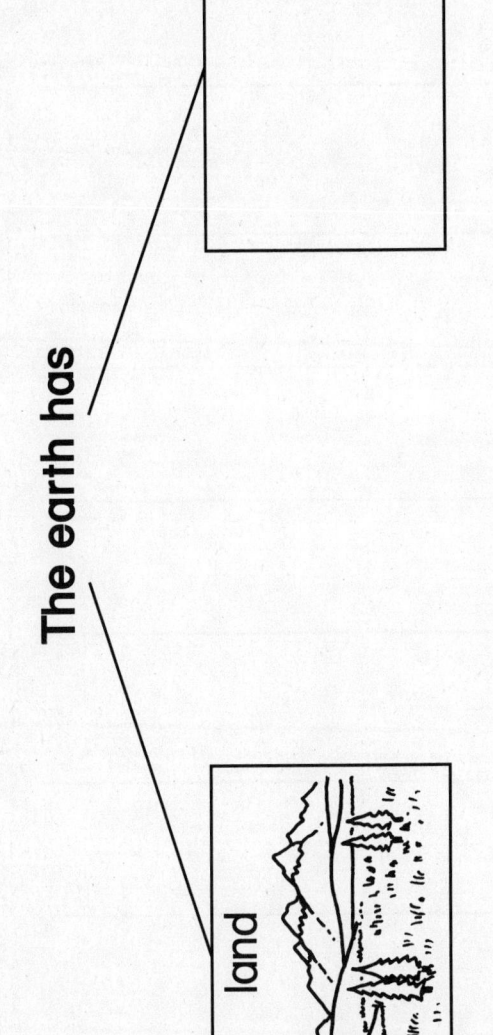

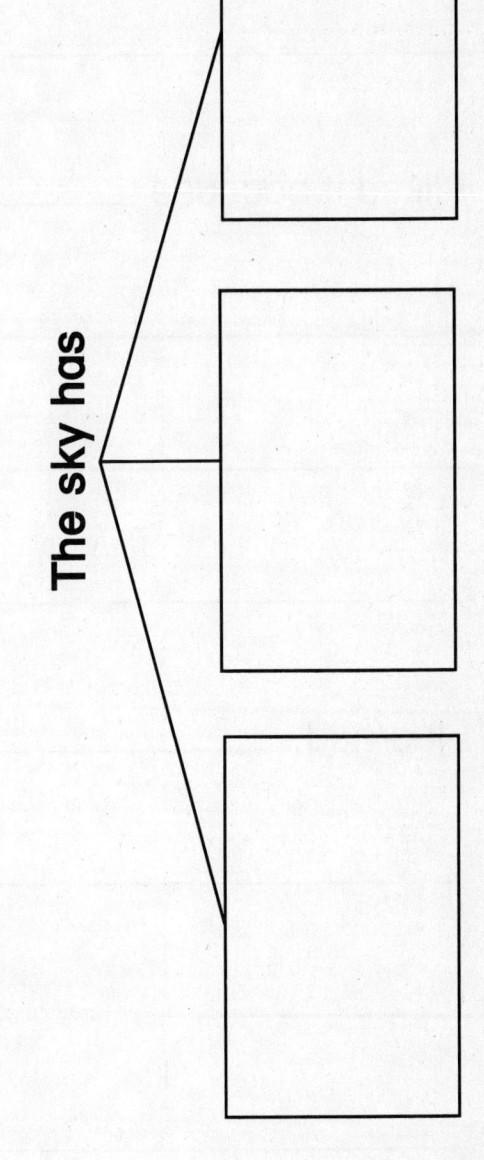

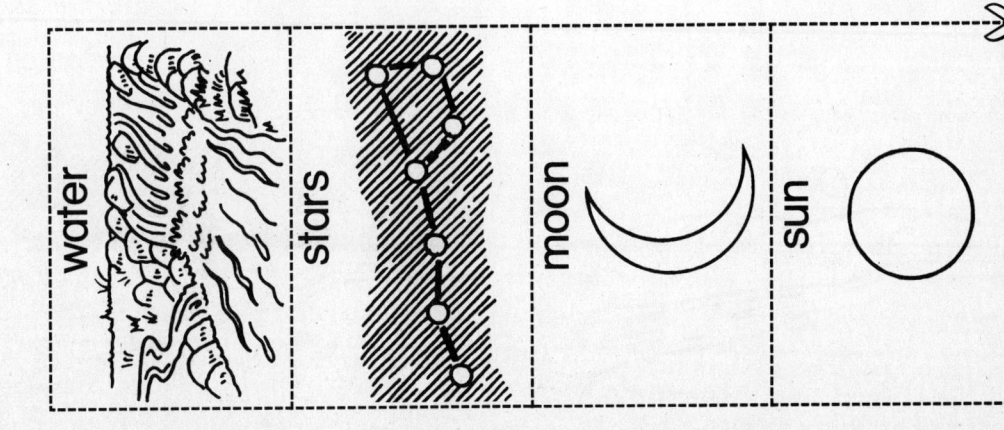

Name _____ Date _____

Graphic Organizer

The earth has

land

The sky has

water

stars

moon

sun

Teacher's Assessment Package

Chapter 1 Graphic Organizer **39**

Name _____ Date _____ **Chapter 1 Review**

This chapter was about _____

_____

I liked it because _____

_____

_____

_____

I learned _____

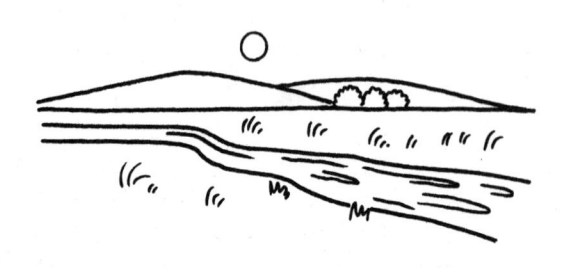

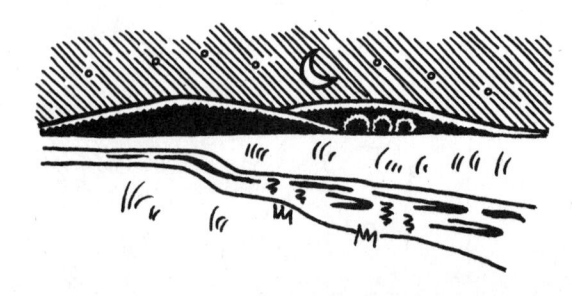

_____

_____

_____

40 Chapter 1 Review　　　　　　　　　　Teacher's Assessment Package

Name _____ Date _____

Chapter 1 Assessment

Look at these landforms. Follow the directions.

1. Color the mountain blue.

2. Color the valley green.

3. Color the plains yellow.

Look at these bodies of water. Follow the directions.

4. Color the river blue.

5. Color the lake green.

Teacher's Assessment Package — Chapter 1 Assessment **41**

Name _____ Date _____

6. Circle the picture that shows early morning.

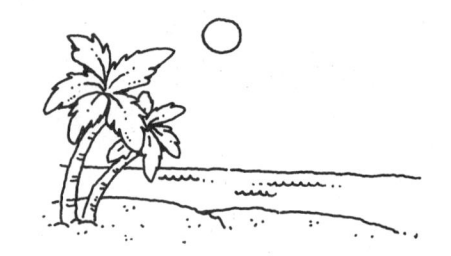

7. Circle the picture that shows midday.

8. Circle the picture that shows the moon.

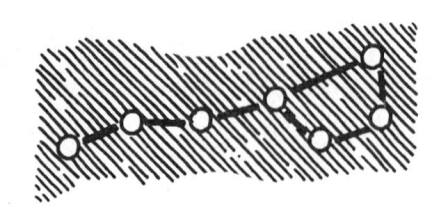

Look at this picture. Follow the directions.

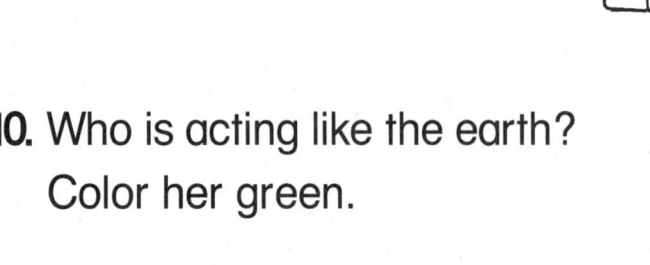

9. Who is acting like the sun?
Color her yellow.

10. Who is acting like the earth?
Color her green.

42   Chapter 1 Assessment   Teacher's Assessment Package

Portfolio Ideas
Unit C Chapter 2

Listed below are items that could be included in students' portfolios for this chapter. The items are categorized by the program component from which they come. Also listed are the main intelligences each item develops. You can use this information to guide students to show their understanding of concepts using their strongest individual problem-solving abilities or intelligences.

These portfolio ideas are only suggestions. You and your students might find other items that demonstrate growing content knowledge, skills development, and attitudes about science.

Component	Item	Intelligence
Teacher's Edition	Pictures from *Topic 1*, p. C17	Spatial; Linguistic
	Picture and poem from *Topic 1*, p. C17b	Spatial; Linguistic
	Weather pattern from *Topic 1*, p. C17b	Logical-Mathematical
	Pictures from *Topic 2*, p. C19	Spatial; Linguistic
	Tape recording from *Topic 2*, p. C19a	Linguistic
	Picture from *Topic 2*, p. C19b	Spatial; Linguistic
	Mural picture from *Chapter Review*, p. C20	Spatial
Student Workbook	What's the Weather?, p. 101	Spatial; Naturalist
	What Will I Wear?, p. 102	Spatial; Logical-Mathematical
	My Favorite Season, p. 105	Spatial; Linguistic
	My Daily Weather Record, p. 106	Spatial; Logical-Mathematical
Teacher's Assessment Package	Chapter 2 Wall Chart, p. 44	Linguistic
	Chapter 2 Graphic Organizer, p. 45	Linguistic; Spatial
	Chapter 2 Review, p. 46	Linguistic
	Chapter 2 Assessment, pp. 47–48	Linguistic; Logical-Mathematical
Interactive Transparency Package	Interactive Transparency 8	Spatial

Name _____ Date _____

Wall Chart

Weather and Seasons

K	W	L

44 Chapter 2 Wall Chart   Teacher's Assessment Package

Name _____ Date _____

Graphic Organizer

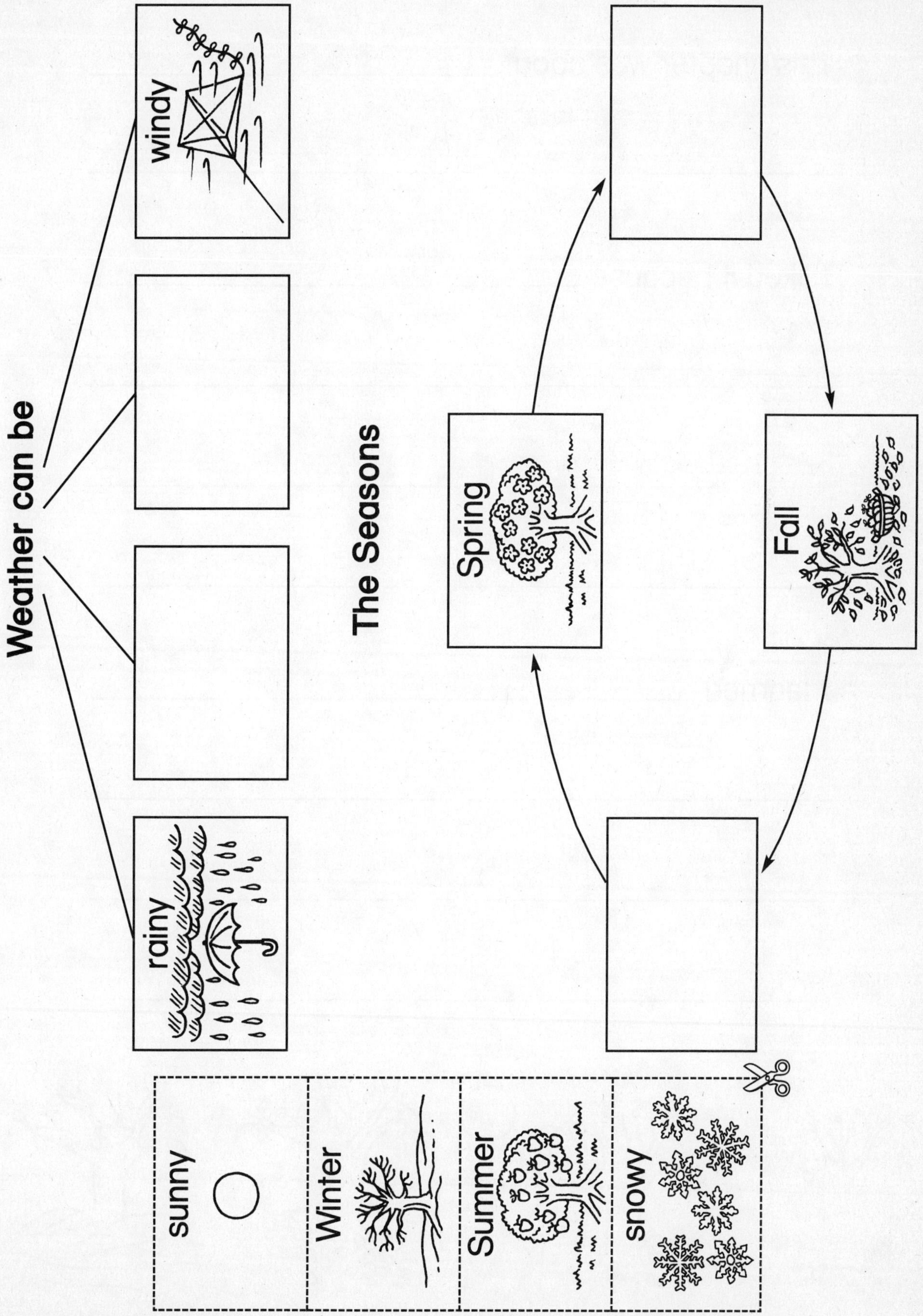

Weather can be
- windy
- rainy

The Seasons
- Spring
- Fall

- sunny
- Winter
- Summer
- snowy

Teacher's Assessment Package

Chapter 2 Graphic Organizer **45**

Name _____ Date _____

Chapter 2 Review

This chapter was about _____

_____

I liked it because _____

_____

_____

_____

I learned _____

_____

_____

_____

Name _____ Date _____

Chapter 2 Assessment

1. Circle the picture of the wind blowing.

2. Circle the picture that shows a snowy day.

3. Circle the calendar that shows a sunny day.

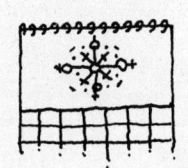

4. Color what you would wear on a warm day.

5. Color what you would wear on a cool, rainy day.

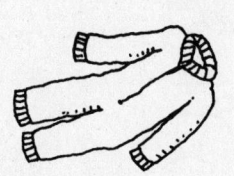

Teacher's Assessment Package — Chapter 2 Assessment

Name _____   Date _____

A garden changes each season.
Draw lines to match.

6. fall

7. summer

8. winter

9. spring

10. Circle what someone might do in summer.

48 Chapter 2 Assessment   Teacher's Assessment Package

Portfolio Ideas
Unit C Chapter 3

Listed below are items that could be included in students' portfolios for this chapter. The items are categorized by the program component from which they come. Also listed are the main intelligences each item develops. You can use this information to guide students to show their understanding of concepts using their strongest individual problem-solving abilities or intelligences.

These portfolio ideas are only suggestions. You and your students might find other items that demonstrate growing content knowledge, skills development, and attitudes about science.

Component	Item	Intelligence
Teacher's Edition	Pictures from *Topic 1*, pp. C25, C25a	Spatial; Naturalist
	Pictures from *Topic 1*, p. C25b	Linguistic; Naturalist
	Pictures from *Topic 2*, pp. C27, C27a	Spatial; Logical-Mathematical
	Headband from *Topic 2*, p. C27b	Linguistic; Naturalist
	Index cards from *Topic 2*, p. C27b	Spatial; Linguistic
	Picture from *Topic 2*, p. C27b	Spatial; Naturalist
	Pictures from *Topic 3*, pp. C31, C31b	Spatial; Linguistic
	Picture from *Topic 3*, p. C31a	Logical-Mathematical
	Recyclable collage from *Topic 3*, p. C31b	Spatial
	Photocopy of How-To Booklet pictures from *Chapter Review*, p. C33	Spatial
Student Workbook	Put Your Stamp on It, p. 111	Spatial; Naturalist
	Ways We Use Wood, p. 112	Spatial; Naturalist
	Energy Pledge, p. 115	Spatial
	Conserving Water, p. 116	Logical-Mathematical
	Let's Recycle!, p. 121	Spatial
	Treasures from Trash, p. 122	Spatial
Teacher's Assessment Package	Chapter 3 Wall Chart, p. 50	Linguistic
	Chapter 3 Graphic Organizer, p. 51	Linguistic; Spatial
	Chapter 3 Review, p. 52	Linguistic
	Chapter 3 Assessment, pp. 53–54	Linguistic; Logical-Mathematical
Interactive Transparency Package	Interactive Transparency 9	Spatial

Name _____ Date _____

Wall Chart

Caring for Earth

K	W	L

Name _____ Date _____

Graphic Organizer

Earth's Natural Resources

- soil
- air

How to Protect Natural Resources

- conserve

forests | recycle | oil | water

Teacher's Assessment Package

Chapter 3 Graphic Organizer **51**

Name _____ Date _____

Chapter 3 Review

This chapter was about _____

_____

I liked it because _____

_____

_____

_____

I learned _____

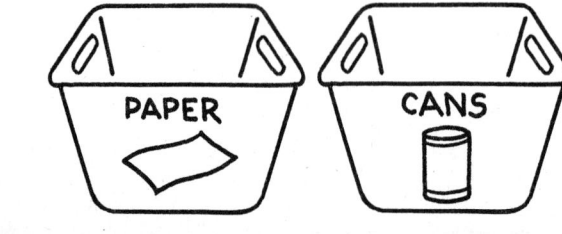

_____

_____

_____

Name _____ Date _____

Chapter 3 Assessment

Circle a natural resource.

1.

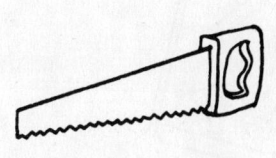

2.

3.

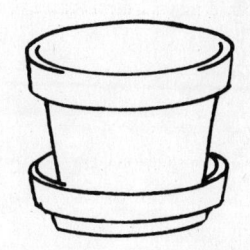

4. Color something made of oil.

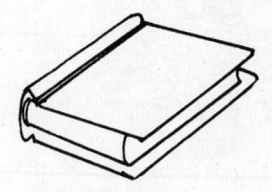

5. Color a way that water is useful.

Name _____ Date _____

Color each person who is conserving a resource.

6.

7.

8.

Circle a way to recycle.

9.

10.

54 Chapter 3 Assessment   Teacher's Assessment Package

Portfolio Ideas
Unit D Chapter 1

Listed below are items that could be included in students' portfolios for this chapter. The items are categorized by the program component from which they come. Also listed are the main intelligences each item develops. You can use this information to guide students to show their understanding of concepts using their strongest individual problem-solving abilities or intelligences.

These portfolio ideas are only suggestions. You and your students might find other items that demonstrate growing content knowledge, skills development, and attitudes about science.

Component	Item	Intelligence
Teacher's Edition	Pictures and sentences from *Topic 1*, p. D7b	Linguistic; Spatial
	Dot painting from *Topic 1*, p. D7b	Spatial
	Pictures from *Topic 2*, pp. D9, D9a	Spatial; Linguistic
	Fragrant Treasure Book from *Topic 2*, p. D9b	Linguistic; Spatial
	Paper plate graph from *Topic 2*, p. D9b	Spatial; Logical-Mathematical
	Picture from *Topic 3*, pp. D10, D11	Spatial; Linguistic
	Picture from *Topic 3*, p. D11	Spatial; Logical-Mathematical
	Alphabet rubbings from *Topic 3*, p. D11b	Spatial; Linguistic
	Picture from *Chapter Review*, p. D12	Spatial; Linguistic
	Menus from *Chapter Review*, p. D12	Spatial; Linguistic
Student Workbook	Ways of Seeing, p. 127	Spatial; Linguistic
	Sounds Around Us, p. 128	Spatial; Naturalist
	What a Smell!, p. 131	Spatial; Naturalist
	Snack Food Tastes, p. 132	Spatial
	Feeling a Mystery Object, p. 135	Spatial; Kinesthetic
	Sorting by Texture, p. 136	Spatial; Logical-Mathematical
Teacher's Assessment Package	Chapter 1 Wall Chart, p. 56	Linguistic
	Chapter 1 Graphic Organizer, p. 57	Linguistic; Spatial
	Chapter 1 Review, p. 58	Linguistic
	Chapter 1 Assessment, pp. 59–60	Linguistic; Logical-Mathematical
Interactive Transparency Package	Interactive Transparency 10	Spatial

Teacher's Assessment Package

Name _____ Date _____

Wall Chart

Your Senses

K	W	L

56 Chapter 1 Wall Chart

Teacher's Assessment Package

© Scott Foresman K

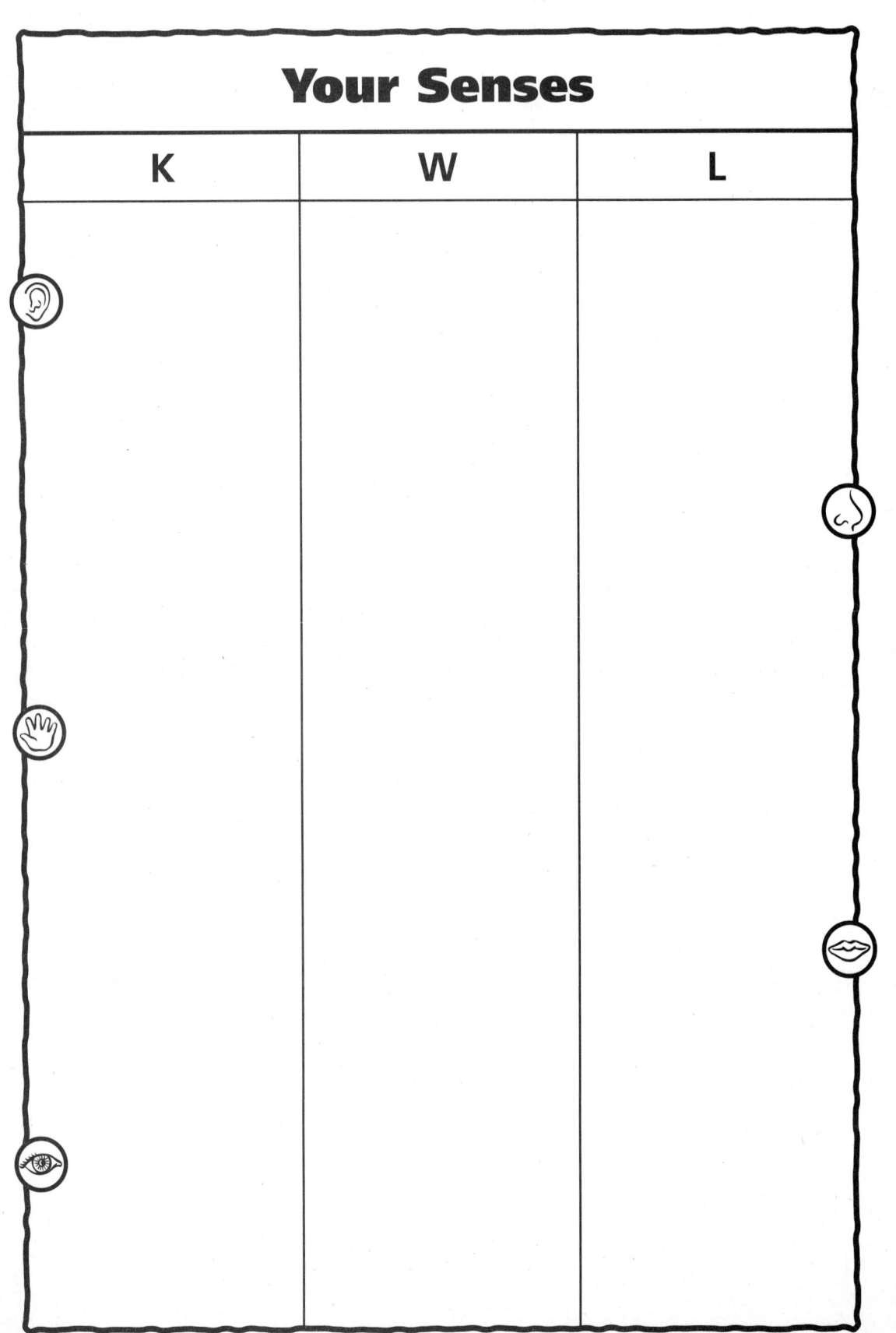

Name _____ Date _____

Graphic Organizer

Your Five Senses

- hearing

---

sight | smell | taste | touch

Teacher's Assessment Package

Chapter 1 Graphic Organizer **57**

Name _____ Date _____

Chapter 1 Review

This chapter was about _____

_____

I liked it because _____

_____

_____

_____

I learned _____

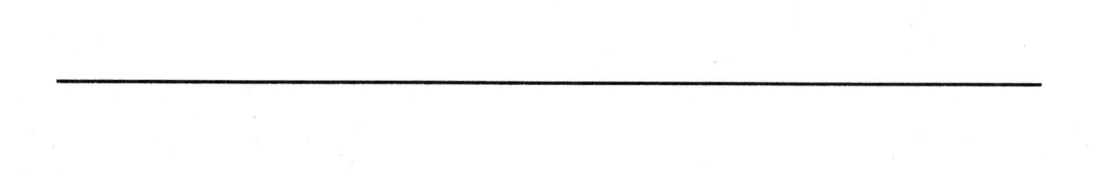

_____

_____

_____

Name _____ Date _____

Chapter 1 Assessment

1. Circle the thing that looks shiny.

2. Circle the thing that makes a loud sound.

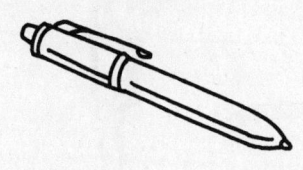

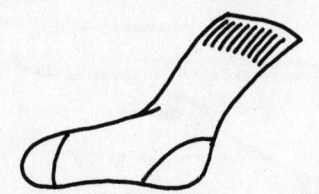

3. Circle the thing that tastes sweet.

4. Circle the thing that has a smell.

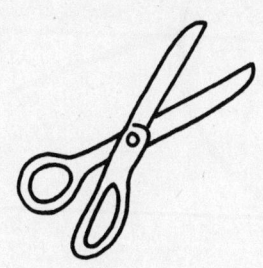

5. Circle the thing that feels soft.

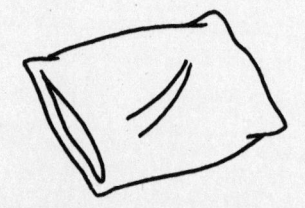

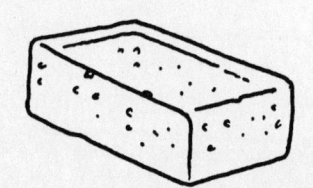

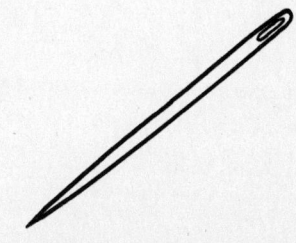

Teacher's Assessment Package   Chapter 1 Assessment **59**

Name _____ Date _____

Draw a line from each sense to the correct body part.

6. touch

7. sight

8. hearing

9. smell

10. taste

Portfolio Ideas
Unit D Chapter 2

Listed below are items that could be included in students' portfolios for this chapter. The items are categorized by the program component from which they come. Also listed are the main intelligences each item develops. You can use this information to guide students to show their understanding of concepts using their strongest individual problem-solving abilities or intelligences.

These portfolio ideas are only suggestions. You and your students might find other items that demonstrate growing content knowledge, skills development, and attitudes about science.

Component	Item	Intelligence
Teacher's Edition	Pictures from *Topic 1*, p. D16	Spatial; Linguistic
	Passport booklet from *Topic 1*, p. 17b	Linguistic; Spatial
	Handprint from *Topic 1*, p. D17b	Spatial
	Pictures from *Topic 2*, pp. D18, D19b	Spatial; Linguistic
	Eggshells from *Topic 2*, p. D19	Spatial
	Shoe and hand tracings from *Topic 3*, pp. D20, D21	Spatial; Logical-Mathematical
	Picture from *Topic 3*, p. D21	Spatial
	Fingerprints and picture from *Topic 3*, p. D21a	Spatial
	List from *Topic 3*, p. D21b	Linguistic
	Picture and sentences from *Topic 3*, p. D21b	Spatial; Linguistic
	Picture from *Chapter Review*, p. D22	Spatial; Linguistic
	Flip book from *Chapter Review*, p. D22	Spatial; Linguistic
	Collage from *Chapter Review*, p. D23	Spatial
Student Workbook	A Puppet Like Me, p. 141	Spatial; Logical-Mathematical
	Using Your Body, p. 142	Logical-Mathematical
	Then and Now, p. 145	Spatial; Logical-Mathematical
	Growing Up, p. 146	Spatial
	Lend a Hand, p. 149	Spatial
	What I Like to Do, p. 150	Spatial
Teacher's Assessment Package	Chapter 2 Wall Chart, p. 62	Linguistic
	Chapter 2 Graphic Organizer, p. 63	Linguistic; Spatial
	Chapter 2 Review, p. 64	Linguistic
	Chapter 2 Assessment, pp. 65–66	Linguistic; Logical-Mathematical
Interactive Transparency Package	Interactive Transparency 11	Spatial

Teacher's Assessment Package

Name _____ Date _____

Wall Chart

Growing and Changing

K	W	L

62 Chapter 2 Wall Chart

Teacher's Assessment Package

Name _____ Date _____

Graphic Organizer

People Grow and Change

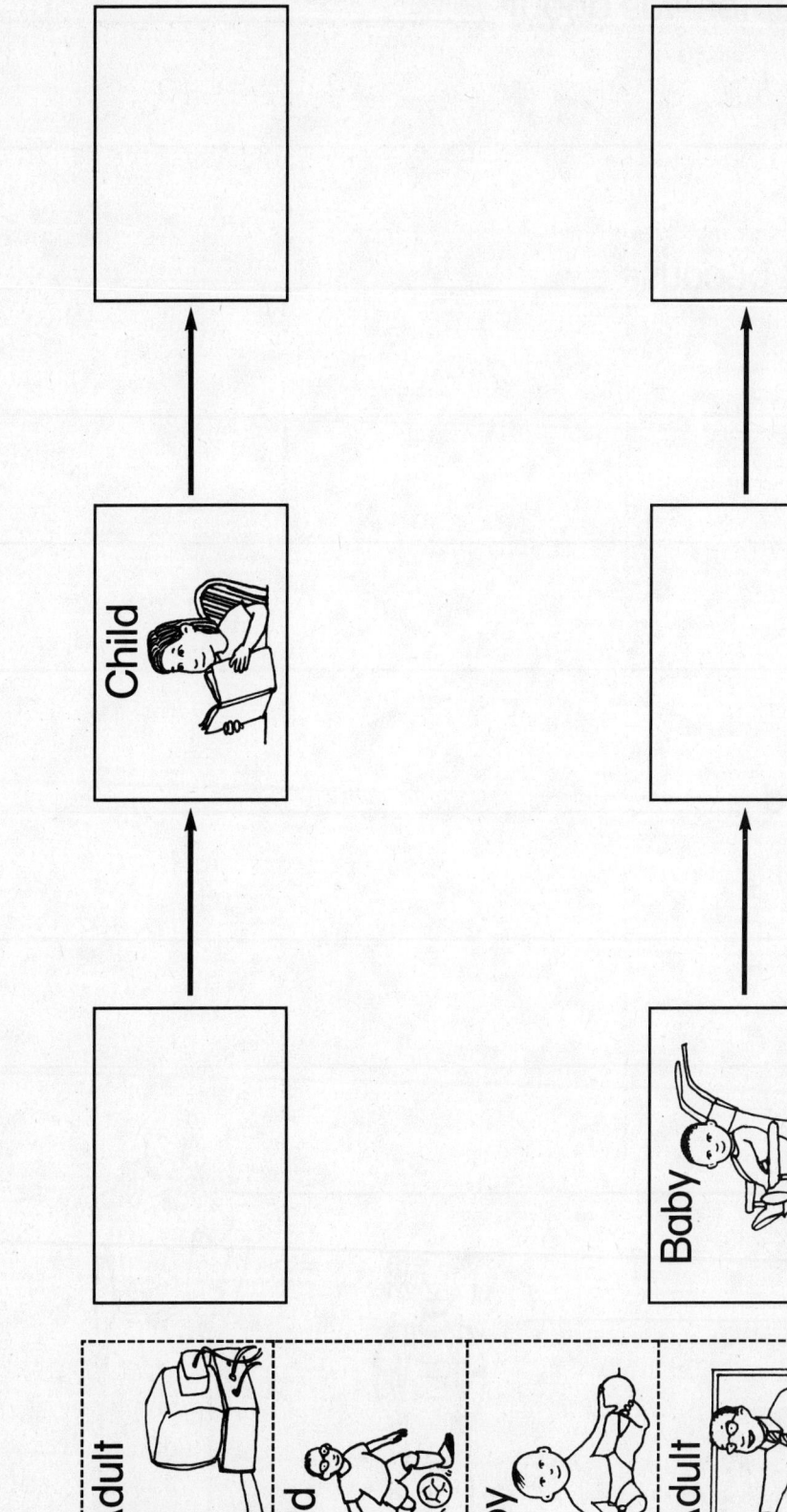

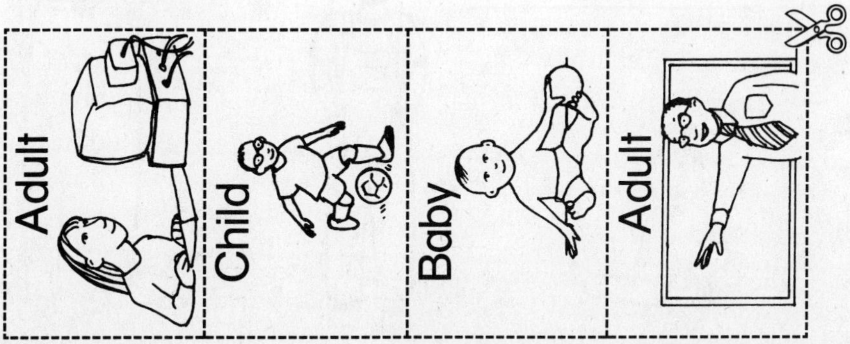

Child

Baby

Adult | Child | Baby | Adult

Teacher's Assessment Package

Chapter 2 Graphic Organizer **63**

Name _____ Date _____

Chapter 2 Review

This chapter was about _____
_____

I liked it because _____
_____
_____
_____

I learned _____
_____
_____
_____

64 Chapter 2 Review

Teacher's Assessment Package

Name _____ Date _____

Chapter 2 Assessment

Look at this girl. Follow the directions.

1. Draw a line to her hand.

2. Draw a line to her leg.

3. Draw a line to her mouth.

4. Draw a line to her arm.

5. Circle the body part you use to clap.

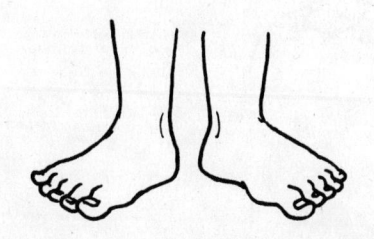

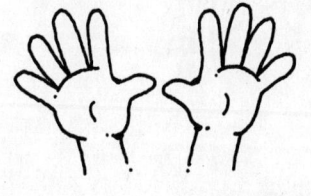

Teacher's Assessment Package   Chapter 2 Assessment **65**

Name _____   Date _____

6. Circle the set of pictures that shows how people grow.

7. Circle something that children your age learn to do.

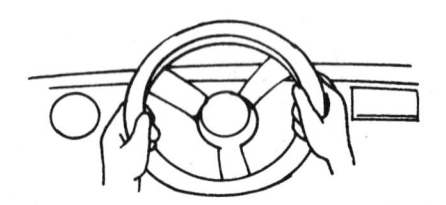

8. Circle the children who look alike.

Circle the person who looks very different from the others.

9.

10.

66 Chapter 2 Assessment   Teacher's Assessment Package

Portfolio Ideas
Unit D Chapter 3

Listed below are items that could be included in students' portfolios for this chapter. The items are categorized by the program component from which they come. Also listed are the main intelligences each item develops. You can use this information to guide students to show their understanding of concepts using their strongest individual problem-solving abilities or intelligences.

These portfolio ideas are only suggestions. You and your students might find other items that demonstrate growing content knowledge, skills development, and attitudes about science.

Component	Item	Intelligence
Teacher's Edition	"Exercise blocks" from *Topic 1*, p. D26	Spatial
	Pictures from *Topic 1*, pp. D26, D27	Spatial
	Pictures from *Topic 1*, p. D27a	Spatial; Logical-Mathematical
	Picture from *Topic 1*, p. D27b	Linguistic; Spatial
	Pictures from *Topic 2*, p. D28	Spatial
	Chart from *Topic 2*, p. D29	Spatial; Linguistic
	Paper plate meal from *Topic 2*, p. D29	Spatial; Linguistic
	Potato booklet from *Topic 2*, p. D29a	Spatial; Logical-Mathematical
	Pictures from *Topic 2*, p. D29a	Linguistic; Spatial
	Chart from *Topic 2*, p. D29b	Spatial; Logical-Mathematical
	Poster from *Topic 3*, p. D32	Spatial; Logical-Mathematical
	Pictures from *Topic 3*, pp. D33, D33b	Spatial; Linguistic
	Pictures from *Topic 3*, p. D33a	Spatial; Logical-Mathematical
	Collage from *Topic 3*, p. D33b	Spatial
	Pictures from *Chapter Review*, pp. D34, D35	Spatial
Student Workbook	Ways to Exercise, p. 155	Linguistic; Bodily-Kinesthetic
	Ways to Rest, p. 156	Linguistic; Bodily-Kinesthetic
	What's for Lunch?, p. 159	Spatial; Logical-Mathematical
	Planning a Meal, p. 160	Spatial, Logical-Mathematical
	Rub and Scrub, p. 165	Logical-Mathematical
	Hidden Tools, p. 166	Logical-Mathematical
Teacher's Assessment Package	Chapter 3 Wall Chart, p. 68	Linguistic
	Chapter 3 Graphic Organizer, p. 69	Linguistic; Spatial
	Chapter 3 Review, p. 70	Linguistic
	Chapter 3 Assessment, pp. 71–72	Linguistic; Logical-Mathematical
Interactive Transparency Package	Interactive Transparency 12	Spatial

Name _____ Date _____

Wall Chart

Being Healthy

K	W	L

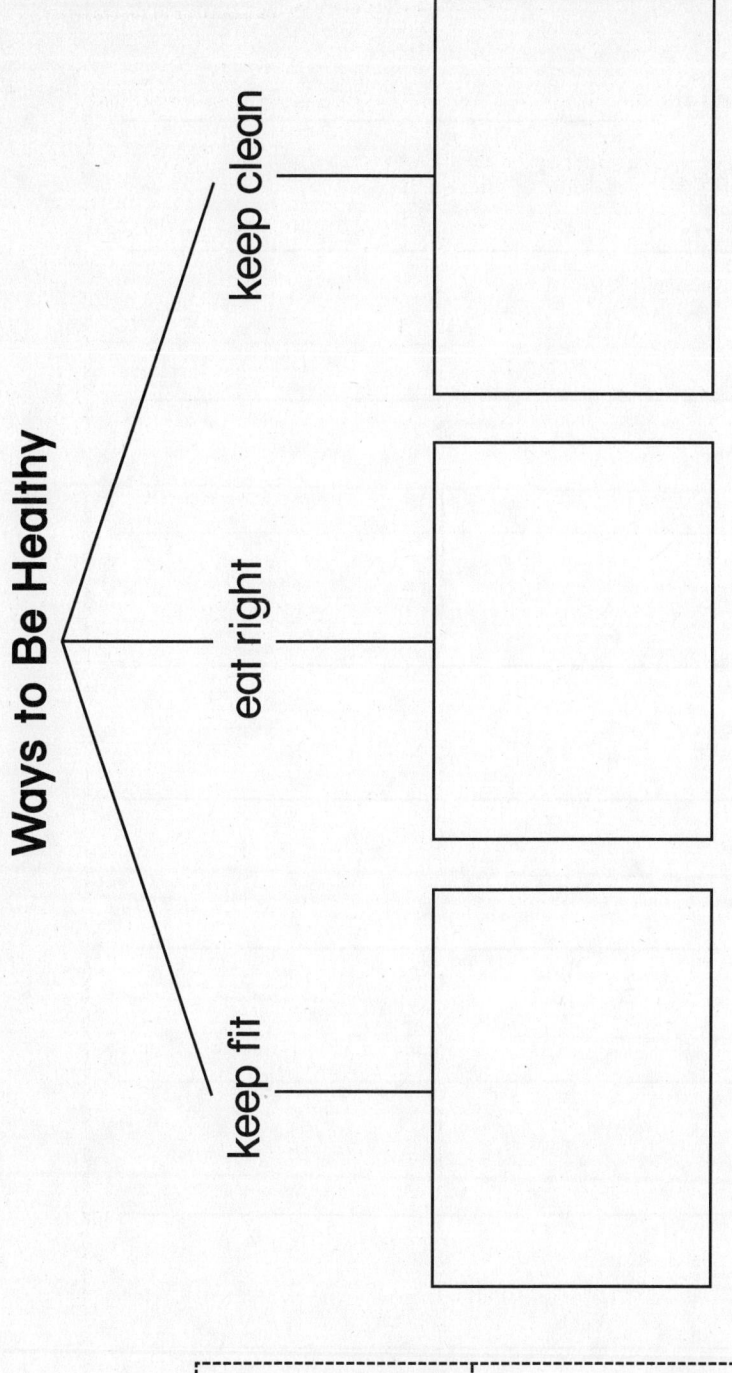

Name _____ Date _____

Graphic Organizer

Ways to Be Healthy
- keep clean
- eat right
- keep fit

- healthcare tools
- rest and exercise
- Food Guide Pyramid

Teacher's Assessment Package   Chapter 3 Graphic Organizer **69**

Name _____ Date _____

Chapter 3 Review

This chapter was about _____

_____

I liked it because _____

_____

_____

_____

I learned _____

_____

_____

_____

Name _____ Date _____

Chapter 3 Assessment

Color the pictures that show people getting exercise.

1.

2.

Color the pictures that show people resting.

3.

4.

5. Circle the food that belongs in the fruit group.

Teacher's Assessment Package   Chapter 3 Assessment **71**

Name _____ Date _____

6. Circle the food that belongs in the grain group.

7. Color the foods you <u>should</u> eat often.

8. Circle the picture if you should wash your hands <u>after</u> you finish.

9. Circle tools used to keep teeth clean.

10. Circle tools used to keep hair clean.

Graphic Organizer

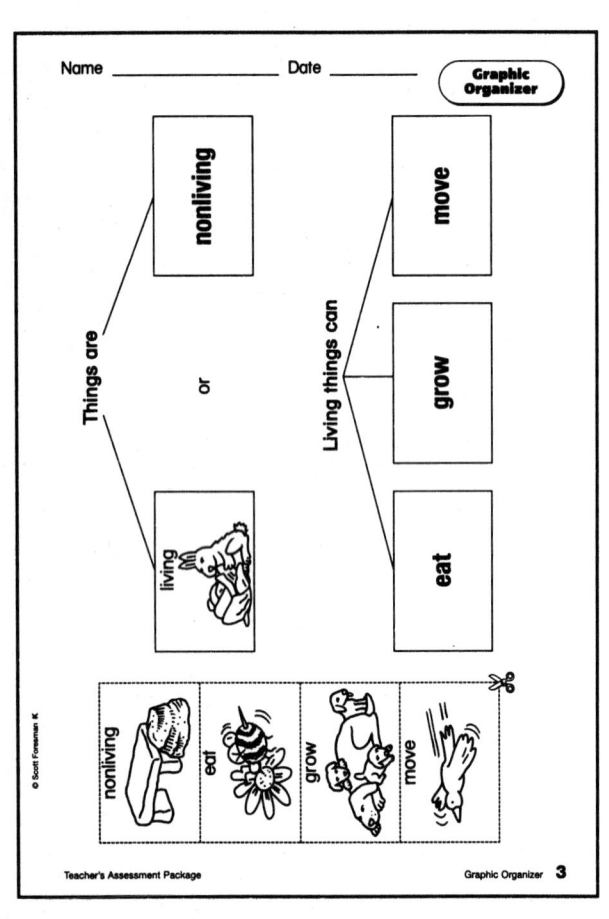

Things are **nonliving** or **living**

Living things can **move**, **grow**, **eat**

Chapter 1 Assessment

1. Circle the plant. *(flowers circled)*
2. Circle the animal. *(raccoon circled)*
3. Which thing can grow? Color it. *(tree colored)*
4. Which thing can move on its own? Color it. *(fishbowl colored)*
5. Which thing can eat? Color it. *(cat colored)*
6. Circle the living thing. *(elephant circled)*
7. Circle the nonliving thing. *(bicycle circled)*

Color the picture that shows what living things need.

8. *(fish food colored)*
9. *(squirrel with acorn colored)*
10. *(dog eating colored)*

74 Answer Key   Teacher's Assessment Package

Graphic Organizer

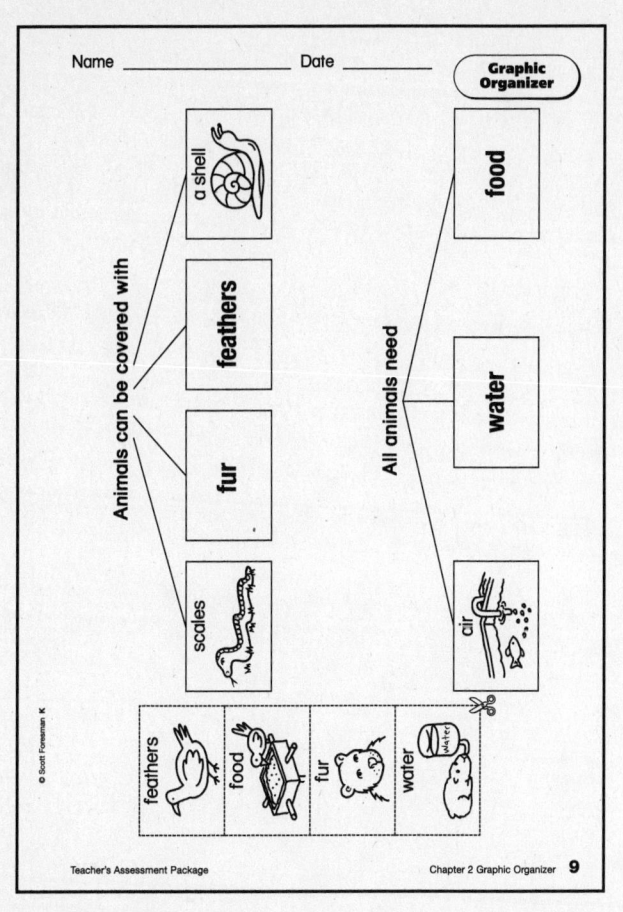

Animals can be covered with: a shell, feathers, fur, scales

All animals need: food, water, air

Cut-outs: feathers, food, fur, water

Chapter 2 Graphic Organizer 9

Chapter 2 Assessment

1. Circle the animal. *(bird with pitcher circled)*

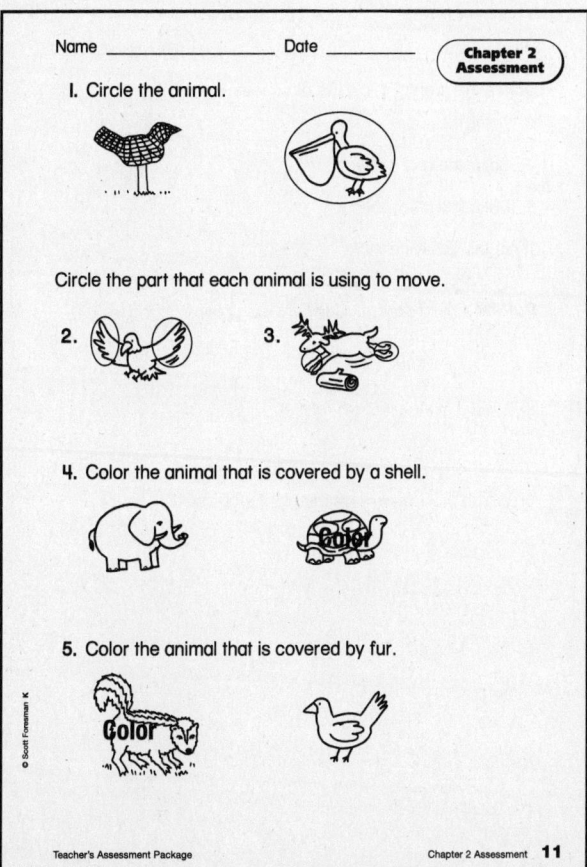

Circle the part that each animal is using to move.

2. *(wings circled)*
3. *(legs circled)*

4. Color the animal that is covered by a shell. *(turtle colored)*

5. Color the animal that is covered by fur. *(skunk colored)*

Chapter 2 Assessment 11

---

6. Circle something that all animals need to live. *(water circled)*

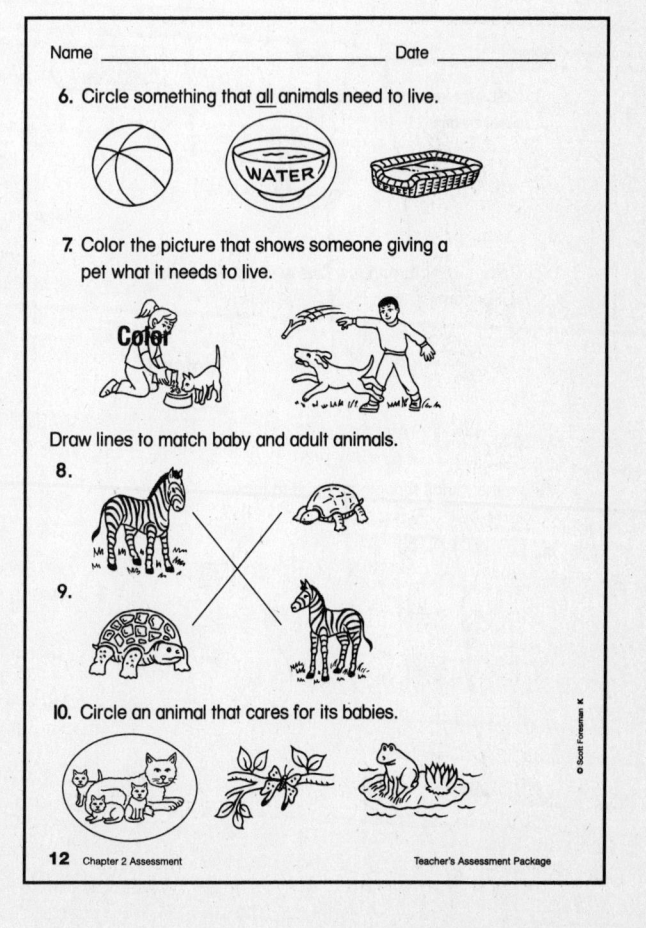

7. Color the picture that shows someone giving a pet what it needs to live. *(girl feeding cat colored)*

Draw lines to match baby and adult animals.

8. zebra — baby zebra
9. tortoise — baby tortoise

10. Circle an animal that cares for its babies. *(cats circled)*

12 Chapter 2 Assessment

Teacher's Assessment Package   Answer Key 75

76 Answer Key

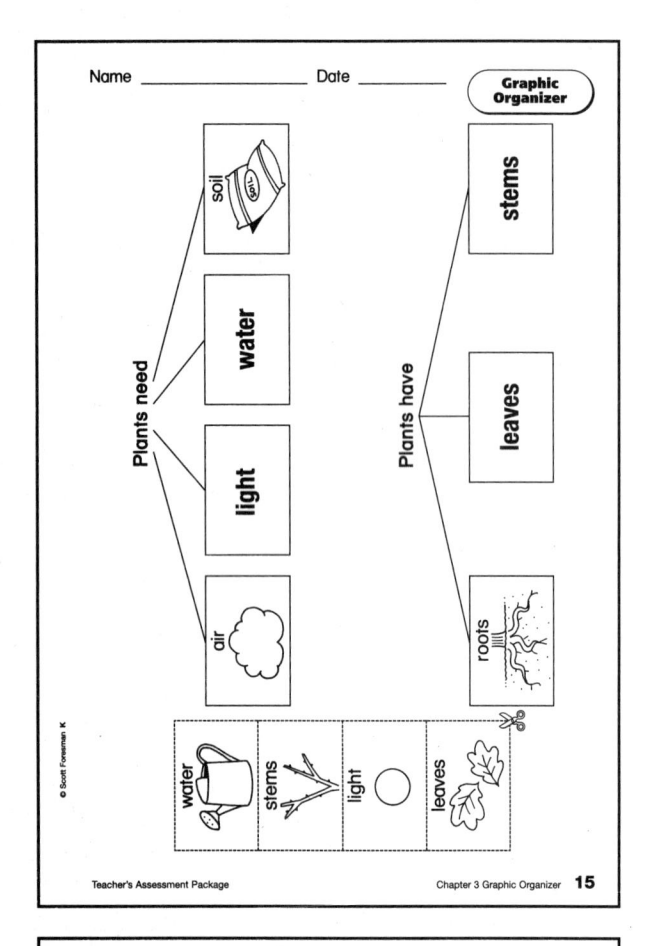

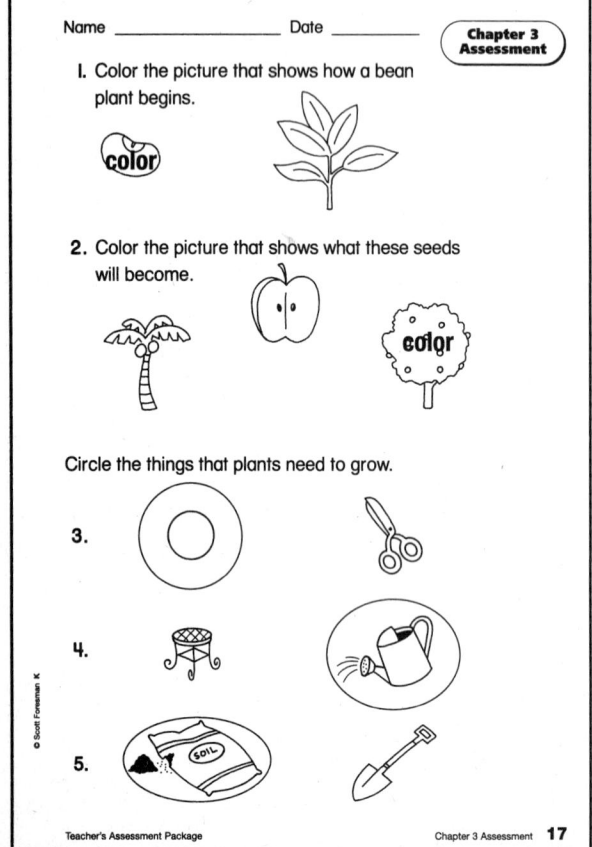

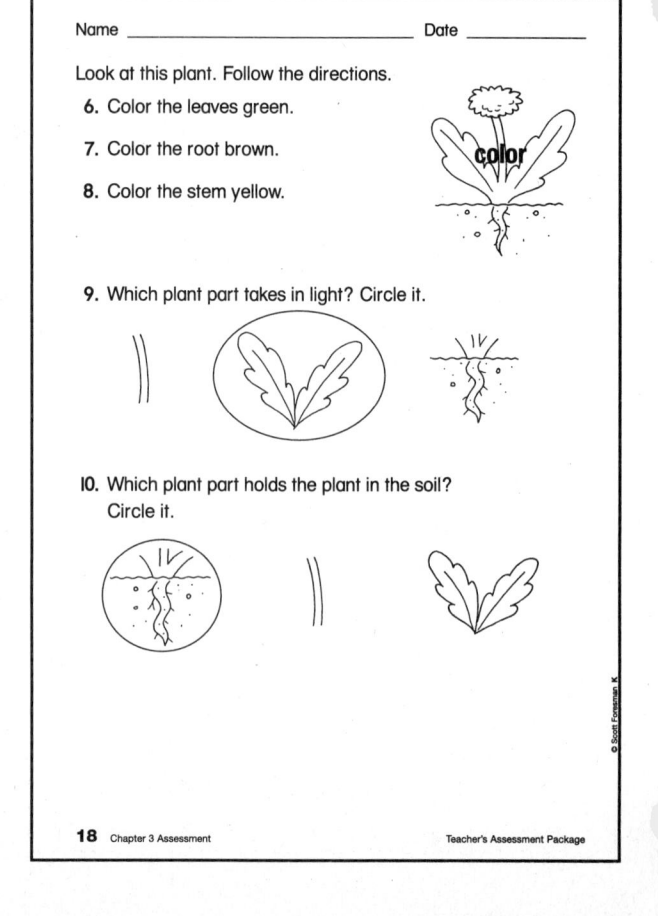

Teacher's Assessment Package

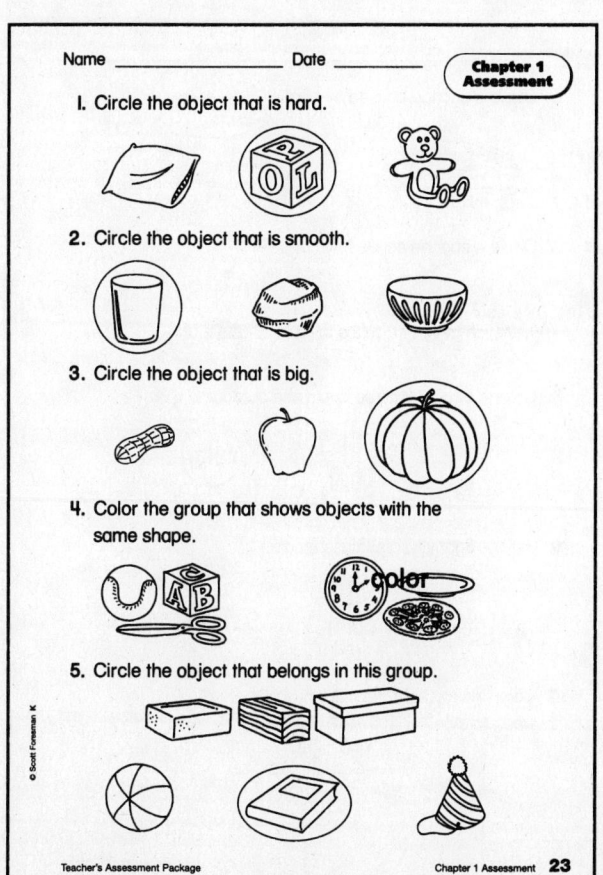

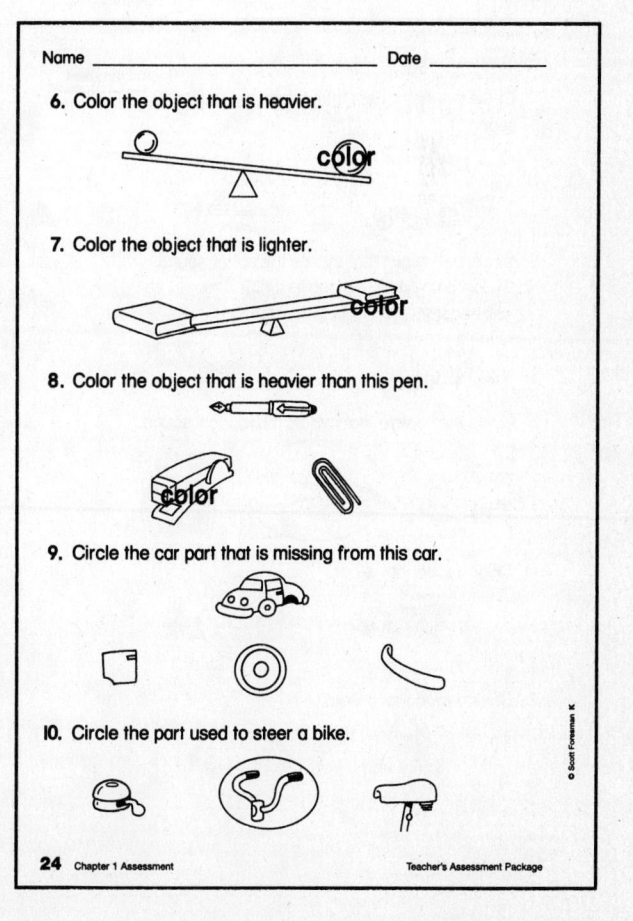

Teacher's Assessment Package

Answer Key 77

78 Answer Key

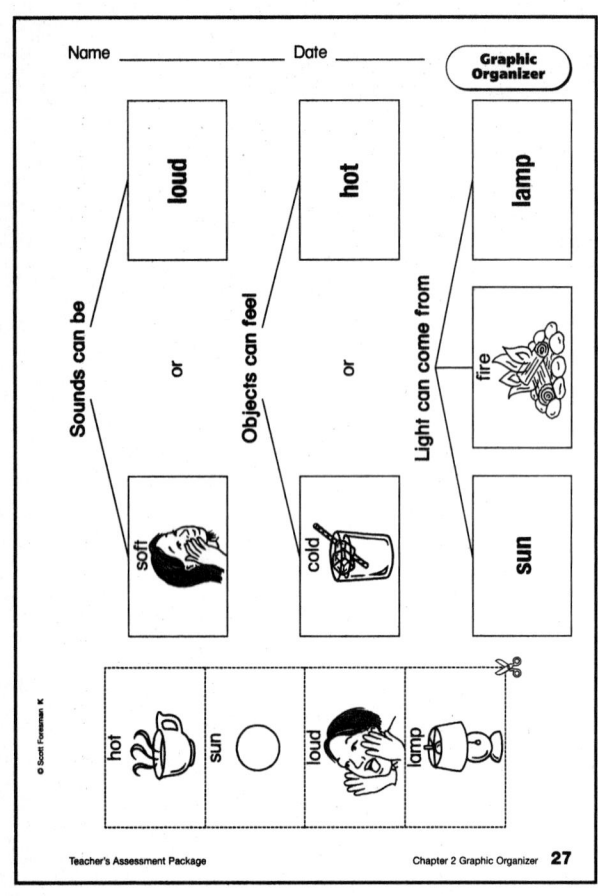

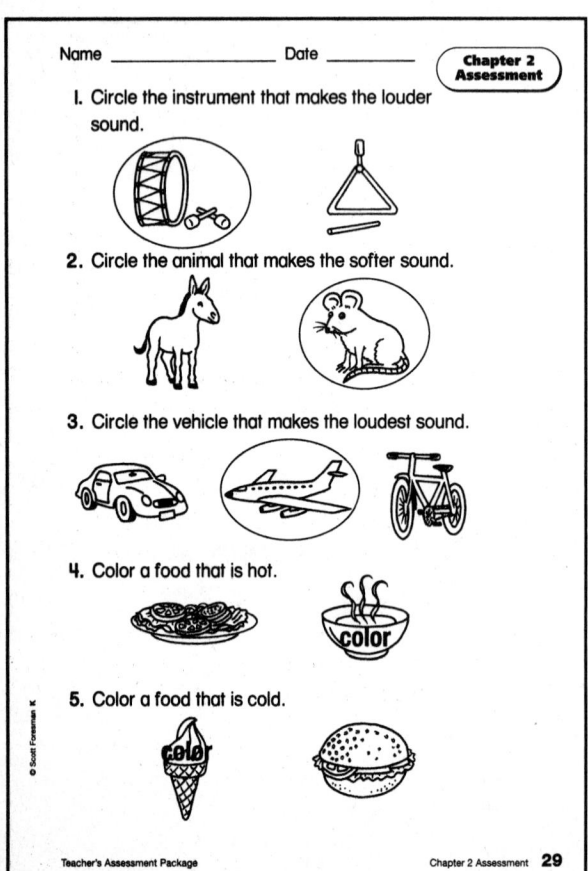

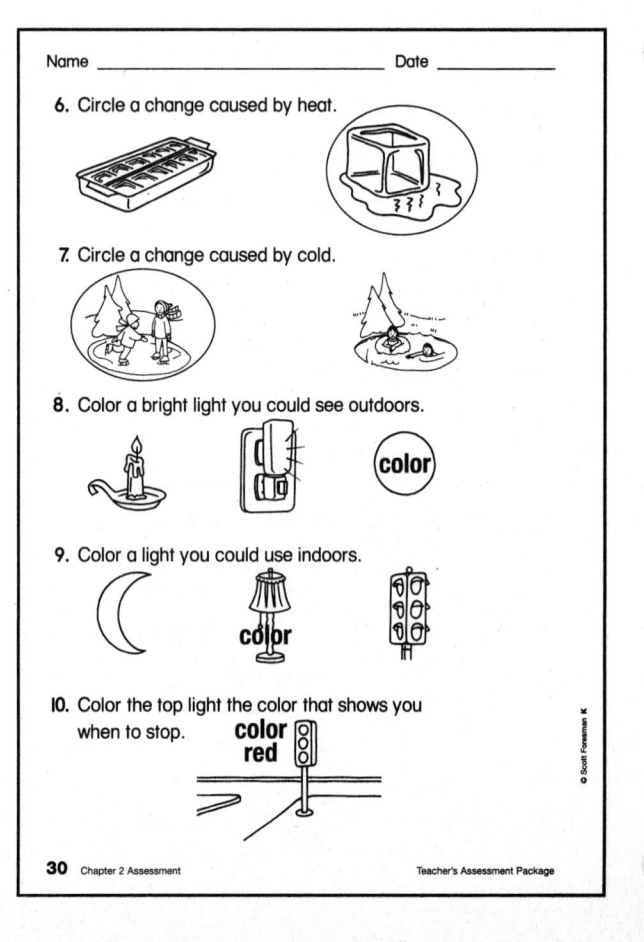

Teacher's Assessment Package

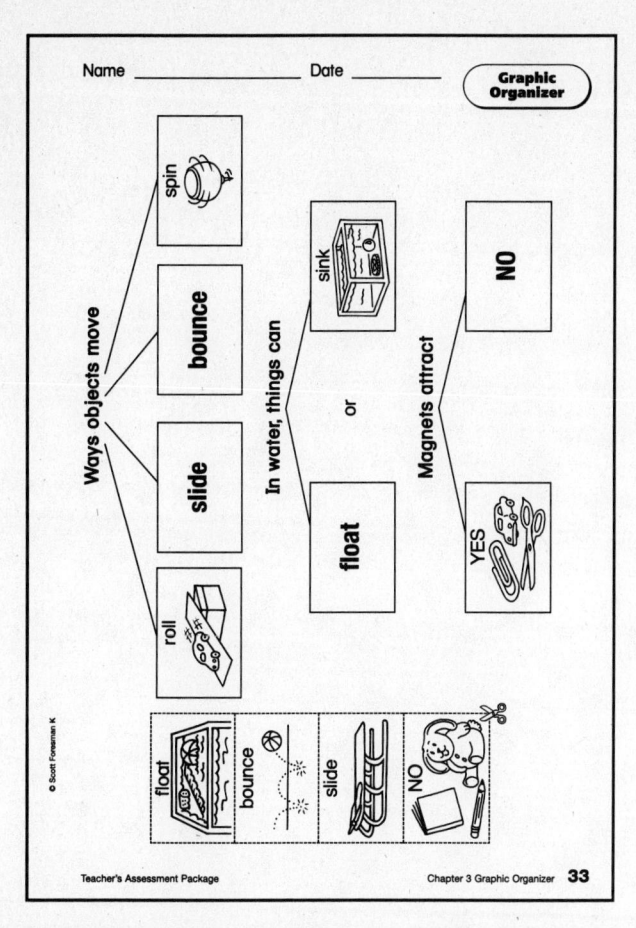

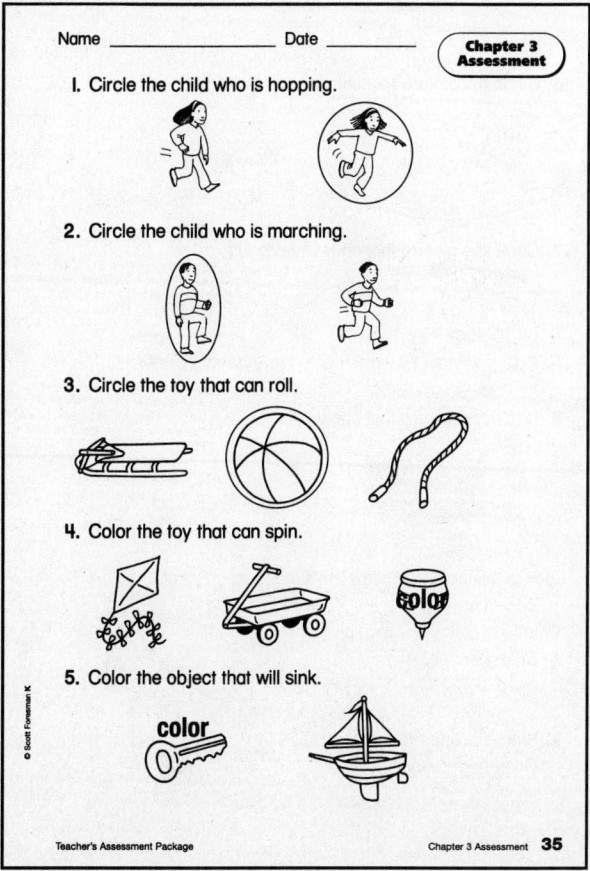

Graphic Organizer

Name _____ Date _____

Ways objects move: roll, slide, bounce, spin

In water, things can float or sink

Magnets attract: YES / NO

Teacher's Assessment Package — Chapter 3 Graphic Organizer — 33

Chapter 3 Assessment

Name _____ Date _____

1. Circle the child who is hopping.

2. Circle the child who is marching.

3. Circle the toy that can roll.

4. Color the toy that can spin.

5. Color the object that will sink.

Teacher's Assessment Package — Chapter 3 Assessment — 35

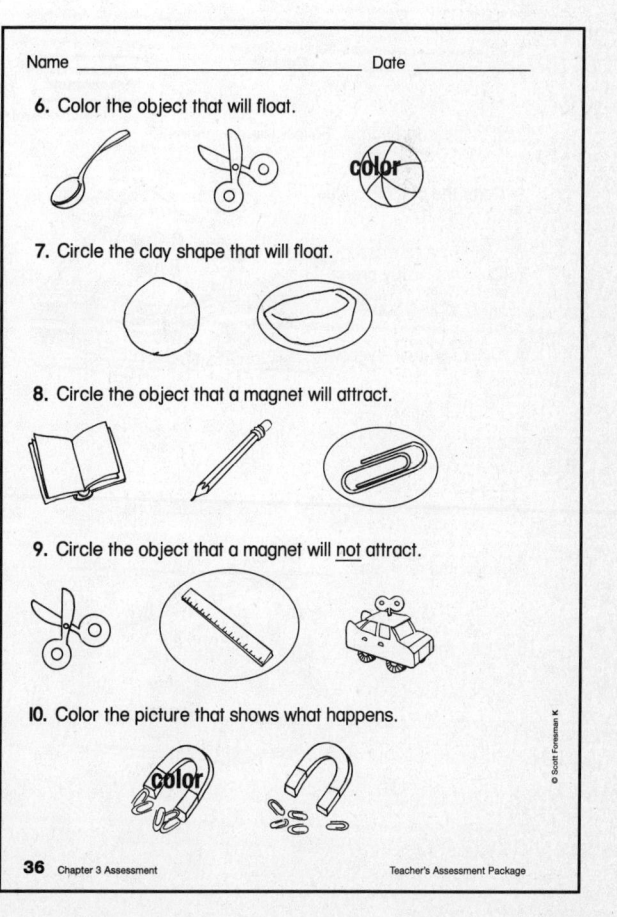

Name _____ Date _____

6. Color the object that will float.

7. Circle the clay shape that will float.

8. Circle the object that a magnet will attract.

9. Circle the object that a magnet will not attract.

10. Color the picture that shows what happens.

36 — Chapter 3 Assessment — Teacher's Assessment Package

Teacher's Assessment Package — Answer Key — 79

Answer Key

Chapter 1 Graphic Organizer (p. 39)

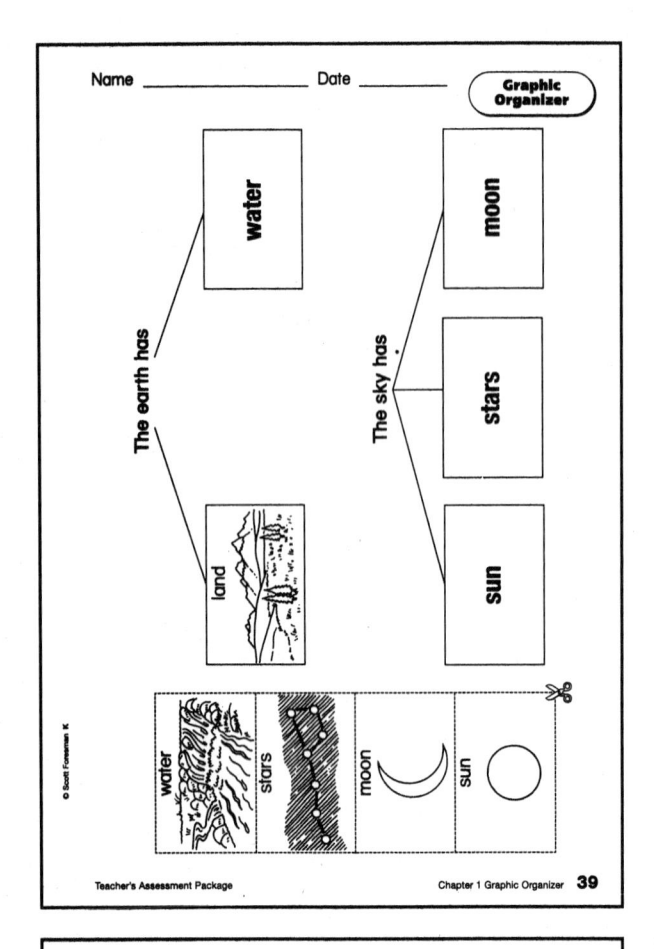

The earth has: water, land
The sky has: moon, stars, sun

Chapter 1 Assessment (p. 41)

Look at these landforms. Follow the directions.

1. Color the mountain blue. — Color Blue
2. Color the valley green. — Color Green
3. Color the plains yellow. — Color Yellow

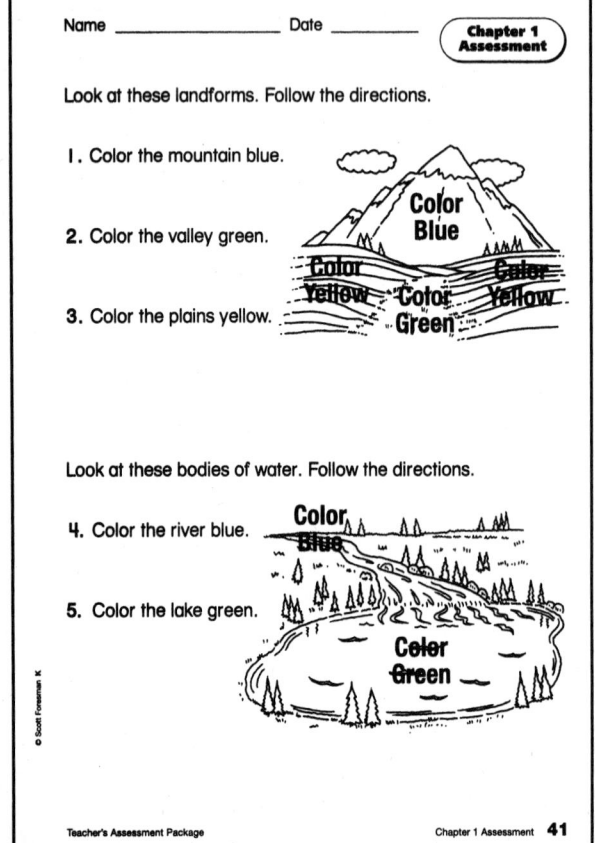

Look at these bodies of water. Follow the directions.

4. Color the river blue. — Color Blue
5. Color the lake green. — Color Green

Chapter 1 Assessment (p. 42)

6. Circle the picture that shows early morning. *(first picture circled)*
7. Circle the picture that shows midday. *(first picture circled)*
8. Circle the picture that shows the moon. *(moon picture circled)*

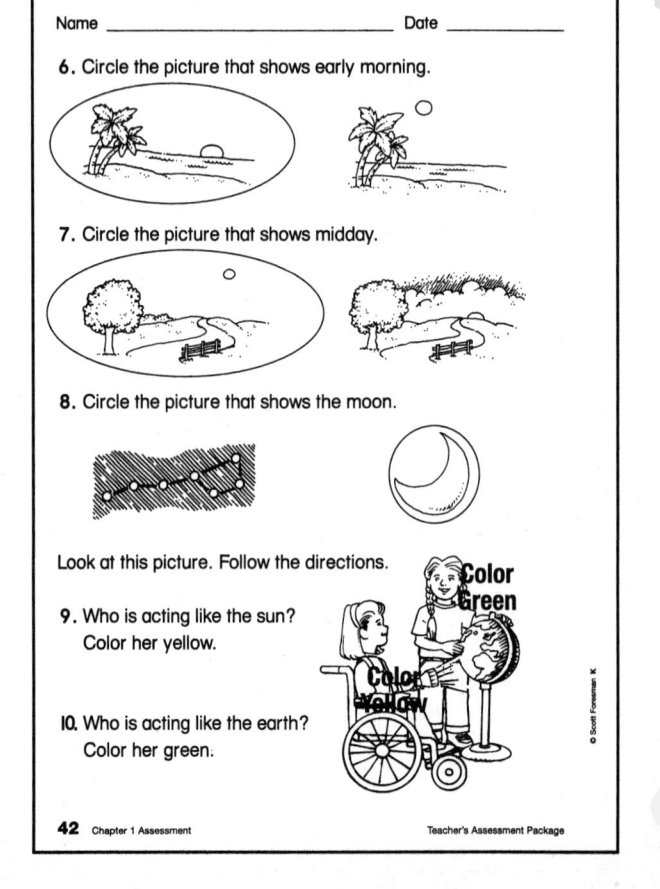

Look at this picture. Follow the directions.

9. Who is acting like the sun? Color her yellow. — Color Yellow
10. Who is acting like the earth? Color her green. — Color Green

80 Answer Key Teacher's Assessment Package

Name _____ Date _____

Graphic Organizer

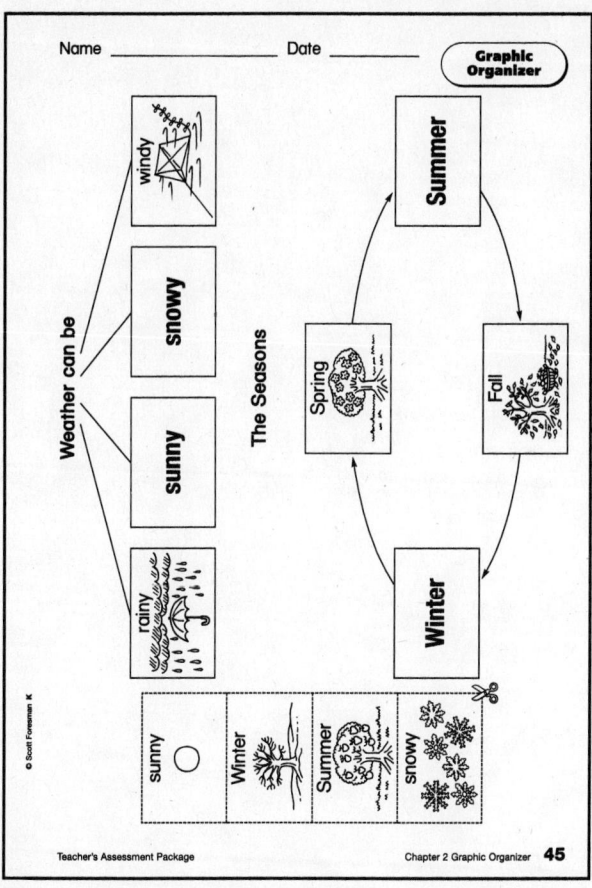

Weather can be: windy, snowy, sunny, rainy

The Seasons: Spring → Summer → Fall → Winter → Spring

[Cut-out pictures: sunny, Winter, Summer, snowy]

Teacher's Assessment Package Chapter 2 Graphic Organizer **45**

Name _____ Date _____

Chapter 2 Assessment

1. Circle the picture of the wind blowing.

2. Circle the picture that shows a snowy day.

3. Circle the calendar that shows a sunny day.

4. Color what you would wear on a warm day.

5. Color what you would wear on a cool, rainy day.

Teacher's Assessment Package Chapter 2 Assessment **47**

Name _____ Date _____

A garden changes each season.
Draw lines to match.

6. fall
7. summer
8. winter
9. spring

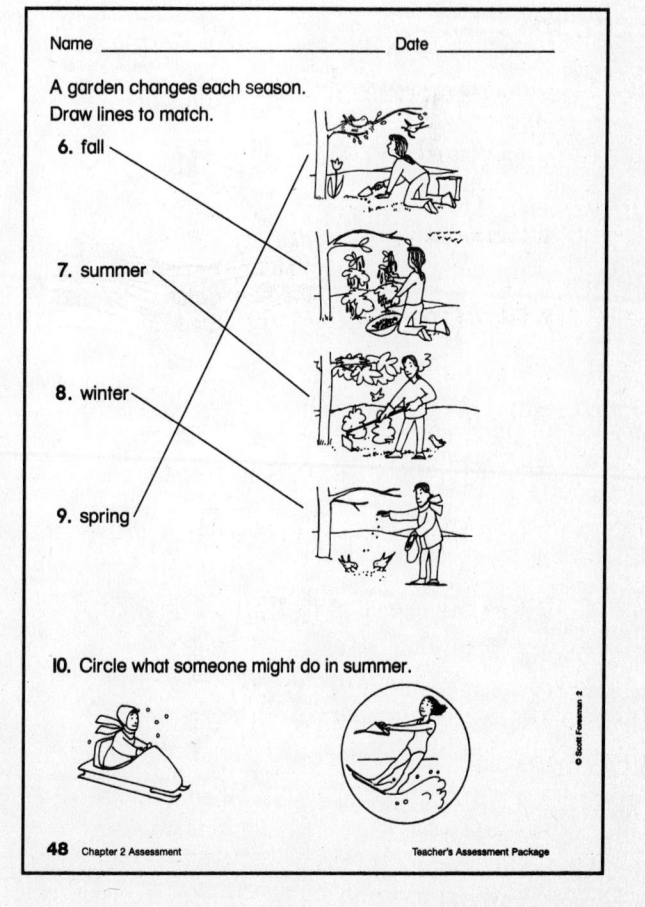

10. Circle what someone might do in summer.

48 Chapter 2 Assessment Teacher's Assessment Package

Teacher's Assessment Package Answer Key **81**

Graphic Organizer

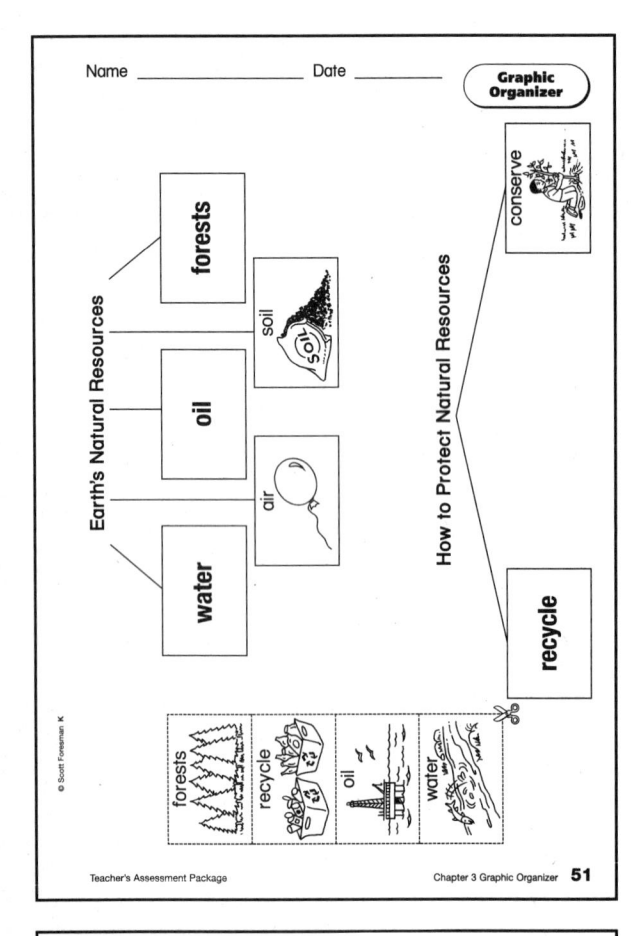

Earth's Natural Resources: forests, oil, water, soil, air

How to Protect Natural Resources: conserve, recycle

Chapter 3 Assessment

Circle a natural resource.
1. (tree)
2. (pond/forest scene)
3. (soil)
4. Color something made of oil. (gas pump)
5. Color a way that water is useful. (child drinking)

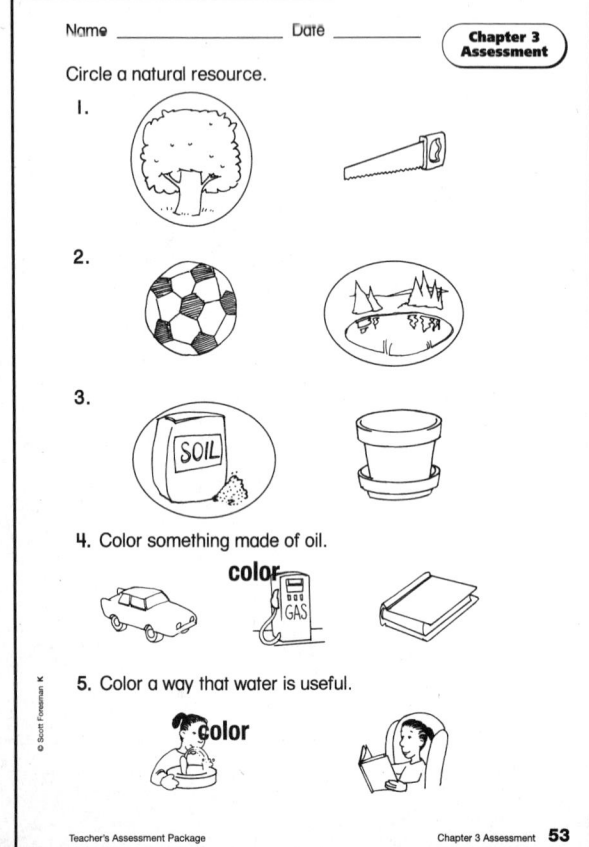

Color each person who is conserving a resource.
6. (bicyclist)
7. (person turning off faucet)
8. (person with reusable bag)

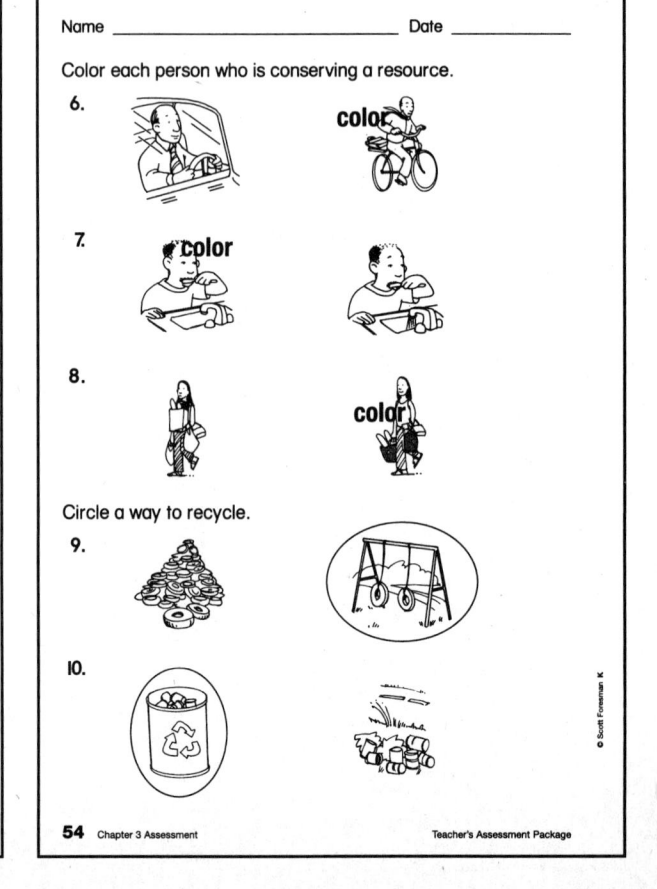

Circle a way to recycle.
9. (cans)
10. (recycling bin)

---

82 Answer Key

Name _____ Date _____ **Graphic Organizer**

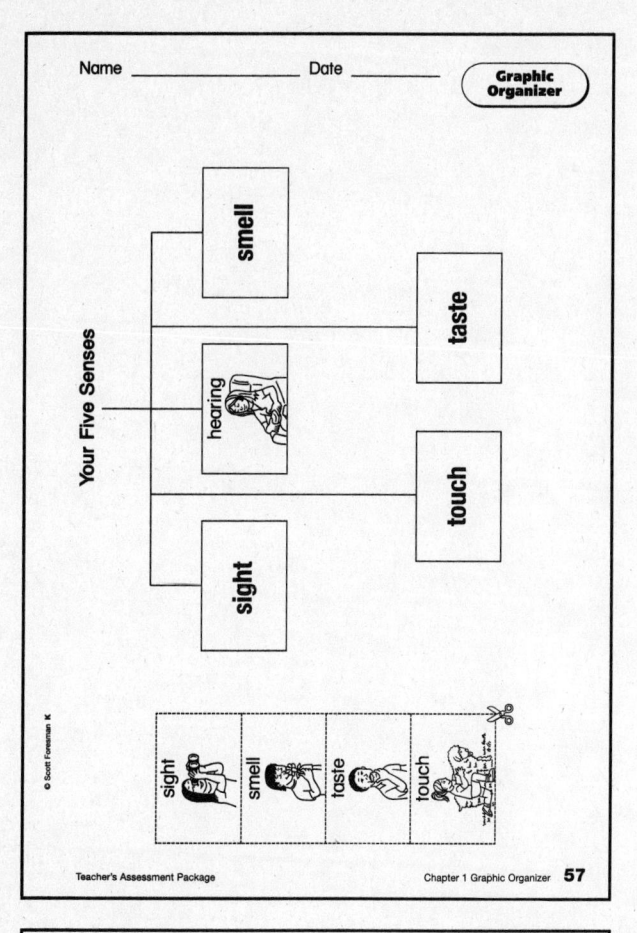

Your Five Senses
- smell
- hearing
- sight
- taste
- touch

sight | smell | taste | touch

Teacher's Assessment Package — Chapter 1 Graphic Organizer 57

Name _____ Date _____ **Chapter 1 Assessment**

1. Circle the thing that looks shiny.

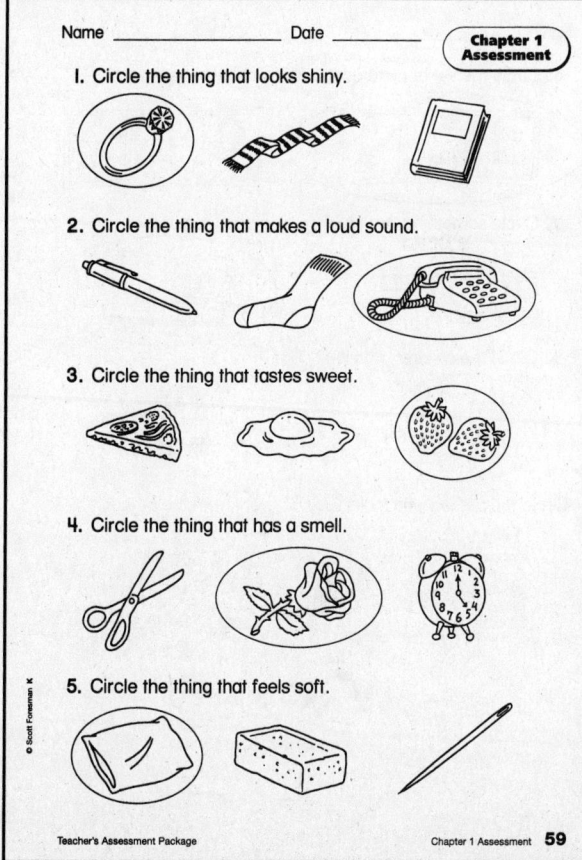

2. Circle the thing that makes a loud sound.

3. Circle the thing that tastes sweet.

4. Circle the thing that has a smell.

5. Circle the thing that feels soft.

Teacher's Assessment Package — Chapter 1 Assessment 59

Name _____ Date _____

Draw a line from each sense to the correct body part.

6. touch
7. sight
8. hearing
9. smell
10. taste

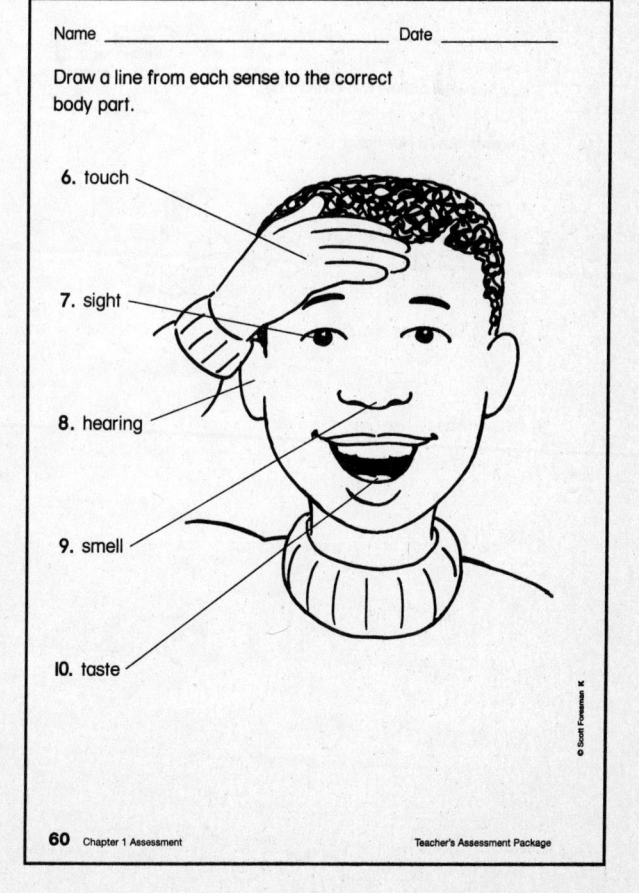

60 Chapter 1 Assessment — Teacher's Assessment Package

Teacher's Assessment Package Answer Key **83**

84 Answer Key

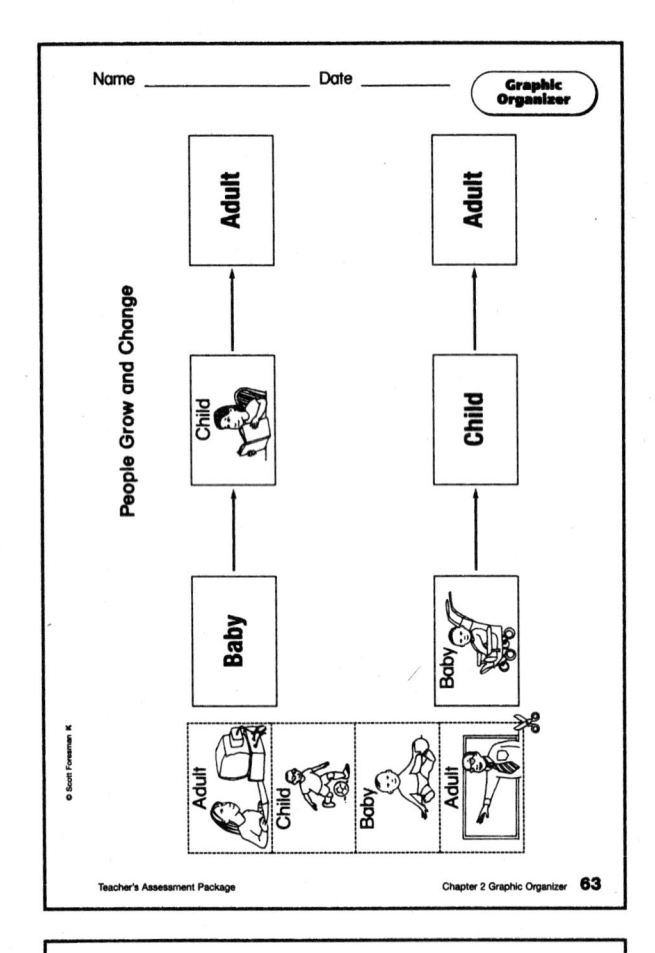

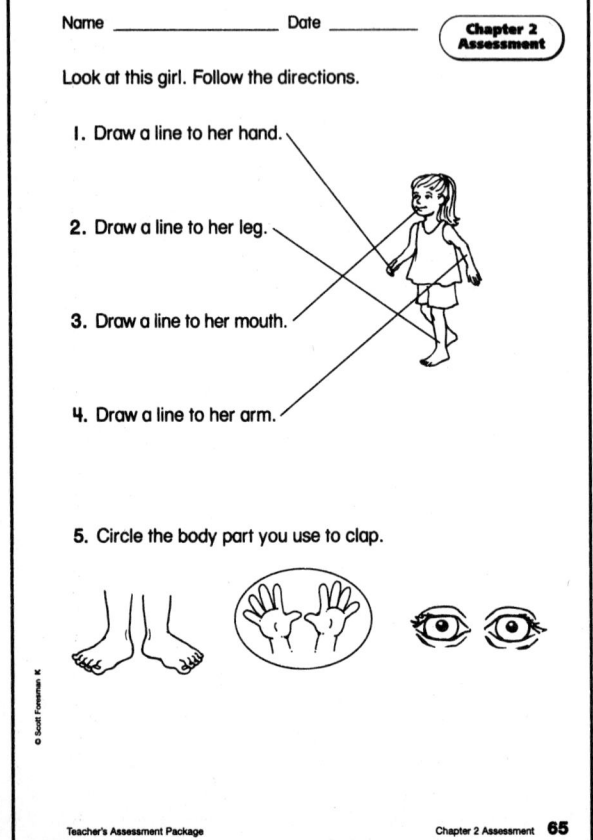

Teacher's Assessment Package

Chapter 3 Graphic Organizer

Name _____ Date _____

Ways to Be Healthy
- keep clean → healthcare tools
- eat right → Food Guide Pyramid
- keep fit → rest and exercise

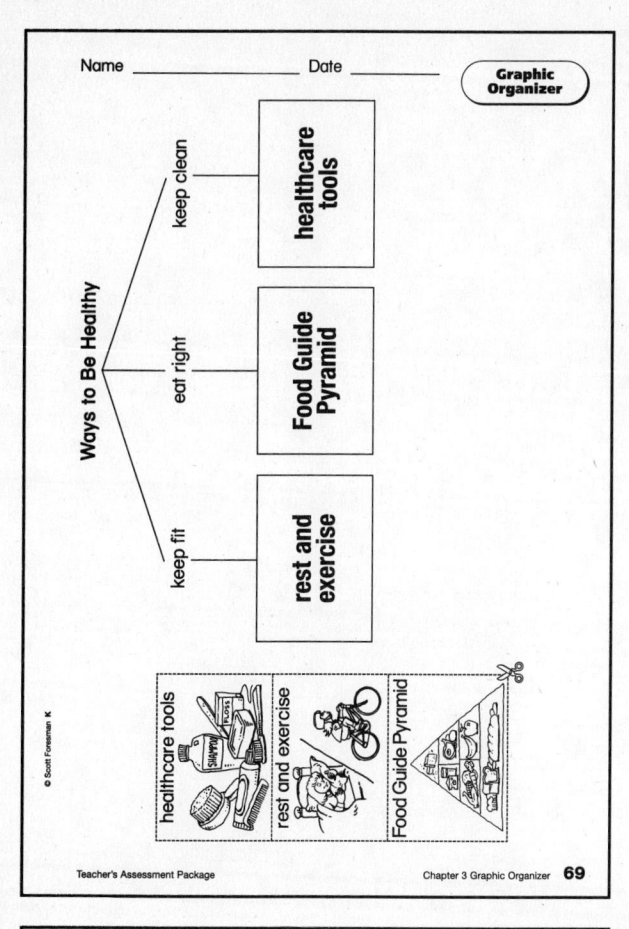

Chapter 3 Assessment

Name _____ Date _____

Color the pictures that show people getting exercise.

1. (girl reading — ; girl with ball — **color**)
2. (boy running — **color**; boy watching TV —)

Color the pictures that show people resting.

3. (boy with dog — ; girl in bed — **color**)
4. (child in hammock — **color**; girl playing —)

5. Circle the food that belongs in the fruit group.
   (milk, **bananas**, eggs)

6. Circle the food that belongs in the grain group.
   (**bread**, ice cream, oranges)

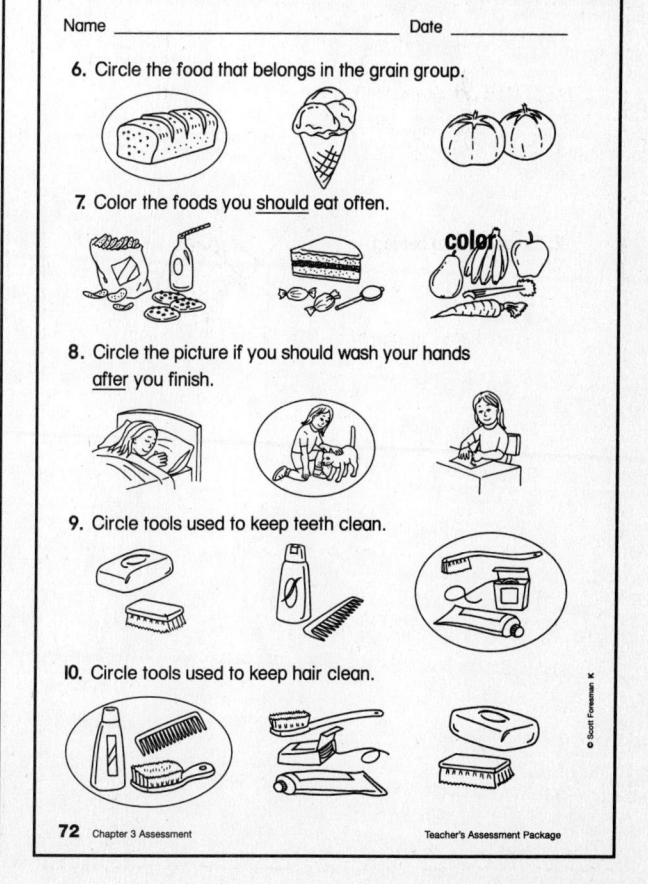

7. Color the foods you should eat often.
   (chips, soda, cake, candy, **bananas/apple/carrots — color**)

8. Circle the picture if you should wash your hands after you finish.
   (sleeping, **petting dog**, writing)

9. Circle tools used to keep teeth clean.
   (soap, shampoo, **toothbrush/toothpaste/floss**)

10. Circle tools used to keep hair clean.
    (**shampoo/comb/brush**, toothbrush/toothpaste, soap/brush)

Teacher's Assessment Package — Answer Key 85